C000132885

WEDDINGS

By James Bentley, Andrew Best and Jackie Hunt

Funerals: A Guide

Weddings

Prayers, Hymns and Readings to Help You Plan the Day

Andrew Best and Jackie Hunt

Hodder & Stoughton

LONDON SYDNEY AUCKLAND

Copyright © 1997 Andrew Best and Jackie Hunt

First published in Great Britain 1997

The right of Andrew Best and Jackie Hunt to be identified as the
Authors of the Work has been asserted by them in accordance with
the Copyright, Designs and Patents Act 1988.

1 3 5 7 9 10 8 6 4 2

All rights reserved. No part of this publication may be
reproduced, stored in a retrieval system, or transmitted,
in any form or by any means without the prior written
permission of the publisher, nor be otherwise circulated
in any form of binding or cover other than that in which
it is published and without a similar condition being
imposed on the subsequent purchaser.

British Library Cataloguing in Publication Data
A record for this book is available from the British Library

ISBN 0 340 65150 4

Typeset by Avon Dataset Ltd, Bidford-on-Avon, Warks

Printed and bound in Great Britain by
Clays Ltd, St Ives plc

Hodder and Stoughton
A division of Hodder Headline PLC
338 Euston Road
London NW1 3BH

Contents

Authors' Preface

When we first embarked upon this book, we thought that the wedding ceremony would be its principal subject. But as we continued, it increasingly seemed that an approach limited to the wedding itself was too narrow for an event that launches two people into one of the most momentous experiences that life has to afford – indeed, into another and very different life, where the needs, hopes and ambitions of one person would in future need to acknowledge another's – in short, the lifelong partnership called marriage.

Much has been written about marriage; its delights, its shortcomings and, particularly, its difficulties. It may seem a little negative to consider, at the outset, the problems of marriage. Weddings, after all, are happy and joyous occasions. But unless the couple embarking upon this life-changing course give some thought to the potential pitfalls of the married state, they are likely to fall into them.

Thus we have tried to find readings that reflect various experiences of marriage down the years. There are many different voices in this book expressing those experiences. Oddly, sometimes it has been a piece from an earlier time that has struck us as being most perceptive and true for our own time.

The wedding ceremony itself may be as short as four minutes (in a register office) or be longer than an hour (a Catholic service including a nuptial Mass). But no matter how short or how long the ceremony may be, the vows exchanged – the marriage itself – are of supreme significance, and spring from traditions older than any Christian church service. The bond of marriage was always important historically for economic and societal reasons. The 'family' was and still is the building block of any society. Without family – no matter how dysfunctional – we have no bonds of loyalty; no cohesion; no possible safe haven for our children (who may eventually find their safe haven within another family).

So any couple about to embark upon marriage should look carefully at the vows to be exchanged and consider what they mean. They are words not to be taken lightly.

But despite this solemn note, a wedding is to be enjoyed. The pieces selected offer, we hope, humour as well as homily, and broadly speaking follow the course of marriage: through courtship and first love, the wedding itself, early marriage, children, the inevitable difficulties, and thankfulness for a life shared.

Andrew Best & Jackie Hunt
London 1997

Introduction

The wedding was very much like other weddings, where the parties have no taste for finery or parade; and Mrs Elton, from the particulars detailed by her husband, thought it all extremely shabby and very inferior to her own. – 'Very little white satin, very few lace veils; a most pitiful business! . . .' But, in spite of these deficiencies, the wishes, the hopes, the confidence, the predictions of the small band of true friends who witnessed the ceremony, were fully answered in the perfect happiness of the union.

JANE AUSTEN, *Emma*

And that is what all of us who venture into marriage hope for – 'the perfect happiness of the union'. Marriage is one of life's great events, and so a wedding is always memorable, no matter how modest our means or how simple the ceremony. The occasion is singular and special not only for the two people making their commitments to one another, but for all those who witness their exchange of vows.

The wedding ceremony may be held in a church, synagogue or temple, in a register office or in a meeting hall. If in a register office or meeting hall – and such a venue can, under recent legislation, be rather splendid, for example, the Royal Pavilion, Brighton; or unusual, for example, the Chelsea Football Club or London Zoo – it is not often that words are spoken other than those legally necessary, nor usual for hymns to be sung or music to be played. But you can make arrangements for additional words and for music and there will certainly be opportunities for both at any gathering afterwards. Alison Cathcart, Westminster's Chief Superintendent Registrar, has said, as reported by Geraldine Bedell in the *Independent on Sunday*, 18 August 1996, that the trend is increasingly towards personalised weddings with music and poetry; Shakespeare's sonnets and Elizabeth Barrett Browning's 'How do I love thee? Let me count the ways' (see pages 109–10 and 161) are particularly popular. She's had a string quartet, a jazz band and even a one-man band. The article continues:

> 'We're having a humanist celebrant because that's the only way we could have exactly what we wanted [The couple are marrying in the garden of her parents' Queen Anne house in the Forest of Dean.] . . . We'll do the legal bit on Friday afternoon – we're trying to make that as unimportant as possible – and then we won't see each other until the wedding on Saturday. We've written the words and we're both musicians so there's a lot of music. We've asked all our friends to bring their instruments. People keep remarking how unconventional this is, but I think it's about as traditional as you can get: at my home, where I grew up, surrounded by family.'
>
> [They] are marrying for themselves and not under pressure from parents, but have found the decision to marry 'has changed people's perceptions of our relationship'. And maybe this helps to explain why marriage remains such a potent idea: it makes everyone feel good.

This couple echo the recommendation made by Helen Wilkinson in her Demos Project Report (1997), *The Proposal: Giving Marriage Back to the People*:

Introduction

> The marriage ceremony as currently regulated by the state leaves the choices too narrow, too antiseptic and too alien to inspire confidence ... I argue for marriage to be given back to the people so that it can better reflect their values.

Our book is not a practical guide on how to plan a wedding. There are many books available (see p. 237), and magazines too, which give advice on etiquette, reception arrangements, food, flowers and fashion, and which indicate the likely cost of a wedding. This book is primarily about weddings as celebrations that mark the personal and social significance of marriage. It includes quotations from a variety of sources which we hope will allow the reader to glimpse the breadth of others' experiences of all phases of marriage, from the thrill and excitement of love and the joy of the wedding itself to a life shared in all its vicissitudes. Many of the readings will be found suitable for reading aloud at the wedding itself, others for quieter contemplation, and there are one or two cautionary tales. There are also suggestions for suitable prayers (pages 36–50), psalms (pages 51–8) and hymns (pages 220–31) that might be sung and music that might be played, though the possibilities for music are infinite and personal tastes differ widely.

Just as weddings are primarily family affairs, so the marriages that ensue – even if they legally end with divorce – both define and strengthen the families involved. Without marriage, the family would lose identity and individuals would lack that vital sense of where, to whom and with whom they belong. This is not to imply that we turn a blind eye to the unhappiness and damage that can occur within marriage and the family, or that we ignore the pain that accompanies divorce. But we must acknowledge that the family is ever-present with us, from birth onwards; the family is the culture that nourishes – however imperfectly – the child's budding ability to experience and to put into practice the cardinal emotions of love, thankfulness and unselfishness, without which the human being withers on the vine and may blight his fellows. Apart from extreme cruelty, abuse and neglect, it is better to know the distant father, the tyrannical mother, the uncaring reckless child than not to know them at all.

> The most powerful social model on which we base our lives is that of the heterosexual couple. The notion of a partner for life is introduced to us from early childhood when we become aware of our individual identity within society. It is then that we experience a split between our private and public worlds, and some of our internal experience becomes repressed. We unconsciously long to find a partner who will meet us in both worlds. As we grow up, we develop hopes, fantasies and expectations that one day we will have someone with whom we can share a special intimacy . . . We read about princes and princesses who at long last meet and live happily ever after. Even when a child grows up with parents who fight frequently and are unhappy in their marriage, expectations of a future happy coupling persist. Some parents may transmit to their children that they married the 'wrong' person, that they are unhappy because of the other person. This does not necessarily stop the child's later desire and search for a partner. The child may come to feel that if she or he finds the 'right' person it will all be different. They may find trust or intimacy difficult but the model of the couple will still be ruling their visions.
>
> LUISE EICHENBAUM & SUSIE ORBACH,
> *WHAT DO WOMEN WANT?*

These days, it has become more common for men and women to live together and have children together, outside marriage. But marriage is different from living together. It comes about when two people make a public commitment one to another, take vows in front of witnesses, and, usually, invite family and friends to join them in celebration of this momentous occasion. Most people once they are married sense a difference in attitudes towards them, even though that difference might be quite subtle and hard to pin down. They are regarded as a couple, a 'pair'; they will be invited to any event not as two separate people, but together; the law treats them differently; families treat them differently; friends treat them differently. This is neither good nor bad – it is an inevitable function of the society in which we live. As Regina Barreca puts it in her *Perfect Husbands (and Other Fairy Tales)*:

> A good marriage is a public bringing together of the various elements in our lives so that there is nothing that is secret, furtive, or vague about our affections. At its best, marriage is a visible and recognizable connection between our every-day lives and the person we love.

In these days of single-parent families, Janet Daley, in the *Daily Telegraph*, 29 October 1996, argues that married couples are likely to provide a better 'moral environment' for children:

> The people most likely to provide such constant, concerned supervision are a child's own parents. It is a simple physical fact that two people can almost certainly accomplish this exhausting, time-consuming relentless task better than one. And two people who have a permanent commitment to one another and to the child are most likely to succeed at it . . . Marriage provides a structure peculiarly well-suited to child-rearing, not because it is unfailingly happy, but because its dissatisfactions and conflicts involve compromise, sacrifice and reconciliation – important lessons to children in how to live with other people.

Marriage does not by itself confer immediate happiness and fulfilment, as many couples have found for themselves. Marriage implies willingness to accept one another's failings as well as qualities; willingness to face difficulties together; willingness to express differences of opinion, accept them, and reach compromises or – most important of all – to agree to differ. All the fundamental aspects of marriage are expressed in the wedding service, even in the short form that is now legally acceptable.

A marriage can be made without a wedding, but no wedding takes place except to celebrate a marriage. So in writing and compiling this book about weddings, we also invite the reader to consider the institution of marriage, the nature of the family and how love between two people who marry can be recognised and sustained. If the wedding can be made apt and memorable, it should endure as a beacon down the years, whatever difficulties and disappointments the couple may undergo.

> The miracle of marriage, if it works, is that it makes you the most important person in the world for at least one other person. Your well-being, your desires and frustrations, your amusements or disappointments matter to your marital partner as they can never matter to anyone else.
>
> DIANA TRILLING, *THE BEGINNING OF THE JOURNEY*

> Marrying, founding a family, accepting all the children that come, supporting them in this insecure world and perhaps even guiding them a little, is, I am convinced, the utmost a human being can succeed in doing at all.
>
> FRANZ KAFKA

'Love makes the world go round' is a robust old saying; it is also a true one. To extend the metaphor: hate impedes it, envy and jealousy divert the planet from its course, selfishness negates it, despair plunges it into perpetual night, and hunger for power threatens to annihilate it.

Without love there would be no family and, without the act of marriage celebrated and made public by a wedding ceremony, family ties would be fatally weakened – and would dissolve away within a few short decades.

Marriage and the wedding ceremony proclaim that the couple love one another, that they express and shall continue to express and nurture their love for one another in the act of love and in other ways, and that their children shall grow up within a family. So the world as we know and love it continues to turn, and those children will marry and have children, and the world will continue to go round.

The engine of love is not, however, confined to Mum, Dad and kids. Love is just as important to the world's turning when it is expressed towards humanity in good works; when it is asexual; when it is homosexual; when it is unmarried love; when it is the love between a single parent and her/his child; and when it is love between a childless couple. Love is what counts; but marriage signifies above all that children may be born, as is their birthright, into a loving family so that they in their turn may learn to love.

> So let us love, dear love, like as we ought;
> Love is the lesson that the Lord us taught.

Yet love can wither and die. Just as we fall in love – and it feels like a miraculous accident – so we can fall out of love. Being in love is a heightened, intensely felt state of being in which the person feels impelled to unite with the object of love, to make love with the love-object and to seek the beloved's company to the exclusion of all others. But sexual ecstasy coupled with a repetitive pattern of behaviour towards one another tends to lose its charms if being in love is the sole impulse towards intimacy. So we fall out of love, soon to fall in love with someone else, and the process may be repeated time and time again.

Without the kick-start of falling in love, most of us would not marry and have children. But a kick-start is not the same as keeping the engine running. Only love can do that, and love is no accident; love has to be recognised as an active principle, it has to be *learnt* and it requires constant practice. Before they marry each other, the prospective bride and groom should try to evolve from the rapturous state of being in love and examine their own feelings and motives.

Unhappily, the word 'love' has two distinct yet overlapping meanings and confusion between the two can lead to misunderstanding, disappointment and misery.

The following statistics are not intended to put you off, but it is surely as well for all who are contemplating marriage to be informed about what seems to be the crisis that the institution of marriage faces at the moment. These facts and figures are taken from the Demos Project Report (1997), already referred to on page 2:

- between 1961 and 1991 Britain experienced a six-fold rise in the divorce rate;

- in 1993 over half of all divorces were granted to people who had not reached their tenth wedding anniversary;

- one in four children in England and Wales are expected to have their parents divorced before they are sixteen;

- in Britain, the marriage rate has halved since the 1970s;

- of those who are marrying, over one third are doing so for a second time;

- the first-time marriage rate is now at its lowest level since 1889; and

- in the UK the last four decades have seen a four-fold increase in the numbers of people cohabiting.

And a Mintel survey, as reported in the *Daily Mail* of 10 May 1997, has this to say:

Marriage is in serious decline, particularly the traditional white wedding. The number of weddings has fallen by 7.5 per cent since 1991. The slide is even more dramatic – down 12.3 per cent – among those marrying for the first time, with a full white wedding.

Neither are the omens good for those who do tie the knot managing to stay together. Mintel claims that fewer than half of newly-weds in 1994 will still be a couple to celebrate their silver wedding anniversary.

The company used Government statistics and quizzed 1,500 people on their attitudes towards the institution of marriage. Half said it was not as important as it used to be, with only four in ten regarding it as the 'ultimate commitment'. A third believed it was a good idea to live together first, with 20 per cent of couples cohabiting – double the rate in 1981. And with one in three marriages now failing, 11 per cent were put off because of the likelihood of divorce. The increased tendency to delay getting married until later in life and the expense of weddings were other reasons given for the slump.

The number of wedding services expected [in 1997] is 324,000. But half will be civil ceremonies that detract from the religious significance. These are held mainly in hotels, pubs, stately homes and even football grounds.

Around 18,000 couples each year choose to marry abroad, with the Caribbean the most popular venue.

Compared to the 1960s the decline is even worse – down 40 per cent. But Mintel believes the rate will start to pick up again by 2001. The number of first-time marriages is expected to continue falling, however, eventually accounting for fewer than 60 per cent of all services.

In spite of all these trends, marriage is still popular. Of young people between sixteen and seventeen years old, 82 per cent still expect to marry. The trend would seem to be to cohabit before marriage (59 per cent of 18- to 24-year-olds, *British Social Attitudes Survey, 1989*); wide acceptance of child-rearing outside marriage; with marriage coming later.

The Demos Project Report confirms that in the 1990s couples value most highly 'emotional intimacy, mutual affection, friendship and sexual fulfilment' in a relationship, and points to the evolution of a new model of partnership between men and women in their relationships where friendship and mutual respect seem to be the key factors.

Samuel Johnson's opinion of marriage is characteristically trenchant:

> Boswell: 'Pray, Sir, do you not suppose that there are fifty women in the world, with any one of whom a man may be as happy, as with any one woman in particular?' Johnson: 'Ay, Sir, fifty thousand.' Boswell: 'Then, Sir, you are not of opinion with some who imagine that certain men and certain women are made for each other; and that they cannot be happy if they miss their counterparts?' Johnson: 'To be sure not, Sir. I believe marriages would in general be as happy, and as often more so, if they were all made by the Lord Chancellor, upon a due consideration of characters and circumstances, without the parties having any choice in the matter.'

In *The Intelligent Woman's Guide to Socialism and Capitalism* (1928), Bernard Shaw wrote:

> If we were willing to trust any political authority to select our husbands and wives for us with a view to improving the race, the officials would be hopelessly puzzled as to how to select . . . There is nothing for it but to let people choose

their mates for themselves, and trust to Nature to produce a good result.

'Just as we do at present, in fact,' some will say. But that is just what we do not do at present. How much choice has anyone among us when the time comes to choose a mate? Nature may point out a woman's mate to her by making her fall in love at first sight with the man who would be the best mate for her; but unless that man happens to have about the same income as her father, he is out of her class and out of her reach, whether above her or below her. She finds she must marry, not the man she likes, but the man she can get; and he is not often the same man.

The man is in the same predicament. We all know by instinct that it is unnatural to marry for money or social position instead of for love; yet we have arranged matters so that we must all marry more or less for money or social position or both. It is easy to say to Miss Smith or Miss Jones 'Follow the promptings of your heart, my dear; and marry the dustman or marry the duke, whichever you prefer'. But she cannot marry the dustman; and the duke cannot marry her; because they and their relatives have not the same manners and habits; and people with different manners and habits cannot live together. And it is difference of income that makes difference of manners and habits. Miss Smith and Miss Jones have finally to make up their minds to like what they can get, because they can very seldom get what they like; and it is safe to say that in the great majority of marriages at present Nature has very little part in the choice compared to circumstances.

What follows poses some questions, and may seem to come a little late. You are, after all, about to be married. But it is always of value and never too late to reassess such an important relationship. Of course you feel you know your partner, but in what terms and at what levels of understanding? You will have found pleasure in each other's company, mutual interests and enthusiasms, and shared hopes and ambitions for the future. You may have lived together as partners for some time. Even so, now is the time to take stock of your relationship, to re-examine your reasons for getting married, and to consider your forthcoming marriage in the context of family and society.

> Never marry but for love; but see that thou lovest what is lovely.
> He that minds a body and not a soul has not the better part of that relation, and will consequently want [lack] the noblest comfort of a married life.
>
> WILLIAM PENN

> Women and men need to move from romance to reality without sacrificing a sense of humour or a sense of self-esteem.
>
> REGINA BARRECA

There are questions which perhaps you should ask yourself. For example, when you say 'I love you', or 'I love you more than anything else in the whole wide world', what do you mean? If these words, so precious to the hearer, arise solely from the state of being in love, they may mean:

- I want to possess you;

- I want to be loved;

- I'd be terribly lonely without you;

- I couldn't be happy without you;

- I feel there's something missing in my life. To get married might fill the gap.

If you mean any one or more of these feelings or impulses, take care. Each *feels* like love, but in fact such feelings are the enemies of love.

- To want to possess another is a symptom of profound insecurity. The person is fearful of allowing the beloved freedom of expression, seeking instead to shackle and stifle the other.

- Children want to be loved. Indeed they need to be loved so that they may learn to love when they grow up. To want to be loved signifies that the person is still a child.

- Loneliness is an affliction that no amount of 'love' can cure. This feeling is an acute form of wanting to be loved. The loving person is never lonely, in this sense.

- This implies that the person derives no satisfaction, pride or joy from any of the activities or pleasures that life affords. How can such a person sustain and renew happiness in marriage? Hermann Oeser has this to say:

  > Those who want to become happy should not marry.
  > The important thing is to make the other one happy.
  > Those who want to be understood should not marry.
  > The important thing is to understand one's partner.

- To marry to fill a gap is a dangerous and self-centred delusion. All that this person can bring to marriage is a nagging sense of dissatisfaction with self. The prospect of marriage may beckon, but marriage of itself cannot be a cure; the marriage is to be made by you and your partner together. As Bathsheba Everdene reflects in Thomas Hardy's *Far from the Madding Crowd*:

  > ... a marriage would be very nice in one sense. People would talk about me and think I had won my

> battle, and I should feel triumphant, and all that. But a husband . . . He'd always be there as you say; whenever I looked up, there he'd be . . . What I mean is that I shouldn't mind being a bride at a wedding, if I could be one without having a husband. But since a woman can't show off in that way by herself, I shan't marry – at least yet.

If any of these are your feelings, you may not yet be 'marriage material' and you may have some way to travel alone (which is not the same as feeling lonely) before you can bring to your partner a love that's likely to endure. Walter Trobisch, in *I Married You*, emphasises the primacy of love in marriage; and even where it may be better not to marry:

> There are three things which belong essentially to a marriage: to leave one's parents, to cleave to each other, and to become one flesh. In other words, there is a legal, a personal, and a physical aspect of marriage. They are inseparable. If you do separate them, the whole thing falls apart.
>
> . . . Love has to precede marriage and sex. It is not marriage which leads to love, but love which leads to marriage. It is not sex which creates love, but love which seeks, among other things, also the physical expression.
>
> . . . The public and legal act of the wedding as well as the sex act create irrevocable facts, while love does not.
>
> An engaged couple may one day feel that they made a decision too soon, that the time was not yet ripe and that their engagement was a mistake. They then have the possibility of breaking their engagement without causing an incurable wound to the partner. For love's sake they can let each other go.

There are other feelings that should be looked into:

- Do you love the other person, or are you simply captivated by appearances?

- If you *are* captivated by appearances (and why not?) do you honestly desire to get to know and to understand the beloved, to embark on life's journey together and stay on board? Might you jump ship if something rocks the boat? Elizabeth Robinson (later Montagu) wrote about her suitor to a Mr Freind in 1742:

  > You men adore the pride, flatter the vanity, gratify the ill-nature, and obey the tyranny that insults you; then [you] slight the love, despite the affection, and enslave the obedience that would make you happy.

- Does the appearance that captivates you make you want to know, understand and love the other person or does it merely bolster your own ego? Elizabeth Robinson again:

  > If ever I commit my happiness to the hands of any person, it must be one whose indulgence I can trust, for flattery I cannot believe. I am sure I have faults, and am convinced a husband will find them, but wish he may forgive them; but vanity is apt to seek the admirer, rather than the friend, not considering that the passion of love may, but the effect of esteem can never, degenerate to dislike ... I have known many men see all the cardinal virtues in a good complexion, and every ornament of a character in a pair of fine eyes, and they have married these perfections, which might perhaps shine and bloom a twelvemonth, and then alas! it appeared these fine characters were only written in white and red.

- Does the appearance that captivates you inflate your self-love? William Blake, in *Songs of Innocence and Experience*, in one verse expresses the dangers of self-love:

  Love seeketh only Self to please,
  To bind another to Its delight,
  Joys in another's loss of ease,
  And builds a Hell in Heaven's despite.

  In the contrary verse, he expresses the way love ought to be, that is active, giving and selfless:

  Love seeketh not Itself to please,
  Nor for itself hath any care;
  But for another gives its ease,
  And builds a Heaven in Hell's despair.

  An English madrigal verse, still on the subject of being captivated by appearances, has the following cautionary tale, as simply expressed as it is profound:

  April is in my mistress' face
  And July in her eyes hath place
  Within her bosom is September;
  But in her heart a cold December.

- Are you under pressure from family or friends to get married? Your parents, in urging you to marry a particular person, may seem outwardly to have your best interests at heart, but may in fact have ambitions or longings of their own which are, to put it bluntly, selfish. Your mother may yearn for grandchildren; your father may value your intended partner's financial success. There may also be pressure from friends and contemporaries. Pressure from friends is often more felt by you than voiced by them. Even so, such pressure can be inexorable if your friends are getting married one by one, and beginning to have children; you may feel increasingly left out, and so more inclined to marry for the sake of marrying than because you have found the person with whom you mean to spend the rest of your life.

• Are you secretly envious of any attribute of your beloved? If you are, then you may become prey to a selfish and potentially destructive emotion which is first cousin to the equally destructive pangs of jealousy. Jealousy 'poisons passion', and, as William Blake powerfully puts it in his *Visions of the Daughters of Albion*, is a symptom of self-love:

> Can that be Love that drinks another as a sponge drinks water,
> That clouds with jealousy his nights, with weepings all the day,
> To spin a web of age around him, grey and hoary, dark,
> That his eyes sicken at the fruit that hangs before his sight?
> Such is self-love that envies all, a creeping skeleton
> With lamplike eyes watching around the frozen marriage bed.

You should also examine and reflect upon your own and the other's behaviour:

• when alone together;

• when with members of your families;

• when at social occasions together.

When alone together, are you self-absorbed, steeped in the

17

beloved's presence, to the exclusion of others and of wider interests and concerns? When you long to make love, are you motivated by the desire for self-gratification?

Are you impatient with, heedless or critical of members of your own and/or the beloved's family? Remember that when you marry you join another family, and that other family now has ties with you. You may find your mother-in-law living at close quarters in her old age.

At social occasions, do you ignore your partner for the sake of other company? Do you flirt with others at parties? Do you and your partner find it difficult to share your reactions after, for example, an evening at the cinema, a concert, or a visit to a picture gallery, or to a book that each of you has read, or after a visit to friends or family?

If your answer to any one of these questions is 'Yes', again you've got some way to travel, and the journey together may strengthen and deepen your relationship and bring you into better relations with family, friends and society. But the journey may also lead to a parting of the ways. If so, that may be the better solution, for your relationship as it stands may be too precarious to survive marriage.

On the other hand, if you can say 'No' to most of these questions, you've every chance of making a successful marriage.

The process of self-examination and of taking a cool look at the beloved before the wedding is certainly a difficult one, and may be painful. Even so, if you do not heed the voices of judgment and reason, you may live to regret it.

The Wedding

Wed is Old English, and means a pledge. The ring is the pledge given by the man to avouch that he will perform his part of the contract.

BREWER'S DICTIONARY OF PHRASE AND FABLE

The giving of a ring is supposed to indicate the eternity of the union, seeing that a circle is endless. Among the Jews the rule was for a maiden to marry on the fourth and a widow on the fifth day of the week – not earlier – and the bride is set on the right in the ceremony, while throughout Christendom her place is on the left. In a Roman marriage the bride was purchased by the bridegroom's payment of three pieces of copper money to her parents. The custom of putting a veil upon the maid before the betrothal was done to conceal her blushes at the first touch of the man's hand and at the closing kiss. Kissing the bride the moment the marriage ceremony ended, though not now prescribed, was formerly an imperative act on the part of the bridegroom. The early marriage ceremony among the Anglo-Saxons consisted merely of hand-fastening, or taking each other by the hand, and pledging each other love and affection in the presence of friends and relatives.

LOVE, COURTSHIP AND MARRIAGE

Preparation for the Marriage

Now there are decisions to be taken and plans to be made. As we've said earlier, this book is not a practical guide, but we do want to highlight certain emotional factors which are part and parcel of the practicalities. If you decide to get married simply and with the minimum of fuss, a good deal of what follows may not apply to you. If you've opted for a civil, register office wedding to be witnessed by a small group of close family and friends, you may want first to turn to p. 32 where we talk about register office weddings. It is now possible to marry in one of more than a thousand buildings licensed by a local authority, and couples can marry in the register office of their choice rather than being confined to the district in which one lives.

Meanwhile, what if you've chosen to marry in a place of worship according to a religious ceremony in the presence of a crowd of guests who will celebrate with you afterwards? Almost 50 per cent of all marriages are conducted in church. A recent survey by One Plus One of couples who had married in church found: ' . . . only a few of such couples were regular churchgoers. The rest were seeking ritual, the language of the prayer book and a sense of the uniqueness – and, in a vague way, the sacredness – of the occasion.'

There are other factors to consider:

- Engagements bring with them a considerable agenda. Not only is there the forthcoming wedding to plan – and it's a bit like a military campaign – but the engaged person's social diary tends to get very full. There is your fiancée's uncle abroad, whom she hasn't seen for ten years, who longs to meet the man his niece intends to marry; your oldest friend who lives in another part of the country whom you're considering asking to be your best man; and various friends and family members on both sides who wish to invite both of you to suppers and parties.

20

• The average cost (1997) of a fully-fledged wedding is £10,000. Is the cost affordable? If it pinches, it may cause friction between families, and friction between the couple. This sum of money, if invested for you at compound interest – let's say you're in your early twenties – until you are age 65 (that is, for forty years), would realise a considerable pension fund. Not very romantic, you may say, but perhaps a practical step to take in these days of uncertainty over provision for sickness and old age.

• Whom to invite can cause heartache and reopen old wounds. For example, the bride's father is divorced from the bride's mother, and has remarried; the mother is resentful. The bride, who gets on well with her father's second wife, naturally wants both her parents at the wedding; but her father fears a public stand-off between his former and present wife, and her mother doesn't want to see her former husband with her replacement at his side. The present wife reluctantly stays away; result: unhappy father of bride. Naturally, one hopes that all concerned can put aside their differences and past pain, attend the wedding and behave in a civil manner for this special occasion.

• Weddings can be exhausting, especially after a hectic engagement period. Apart from the months of pre-paration, the day itself can unfold into something like this: after hairdressing, dressing and make-up, the bride and bridesmaids are ready to come to church at 4.00 p.m. on a summer's day. The groom's programme is less demanding, but during the morning he may have been nursing a hangover after carousing with his friends the night before. Then:

4.00 – 4.45	Wedding ceremony
4.45 – 5.30	Photographs, video, etc.
5.30 – 6.00	Travel to reception, assemble guests
6.00 – 8.00	Mingle over drinks
8.00 – 11.00	Sit-down dinner plus speeches
11.00 – early a.m.	Dancing

Total: ten or more hours (not counting dressing, etc.), at least six of which will be spent on your feet!

- A honeymoon or its equivalent is essential afterwards, even if it can only be a long weekend away, so that you can relish being on your own together as a married couple for the first time, and enjoy a well-earned rest and change of scene.

The demanding schedule of the wedding itself, and the sometimes taxing preamble to it, can be put into its proper context and perspective by giving your full understanding to and concentration upon the marriage service itself – before, during and after. Time is an inexorable taskmaster, and too often we are its servants, even its slaves. But the marriage service takes us out of time's prison and affords a glimpse of the eternal. To understand its meaning and to intend actively to fulfil that meaning in your married life will help you to sail serenely through your great day and on into the future.

The night before the day of our wedding
I dreamed that the universe had a party,
All the stars were invited,
Beneath sparkling chandeliers, the planets rejoiced;

In all its beautiful, candle-lit galaxies,
Crowded with glass-clinking revellers,
The Cosmos was Laughing with
Lasting Love and Light.

KATE FARRELL

The Marriage Service

Essentially, you *are* the marriage. Your marriage is made by you, by your exchange of vows in the presence of witnesses. This is as true of the religious ceremony as it is of the civil one. Your marriage is ratified by them according to law. The officiating minister, priest or rabbi does not marry you; you marry each other. The celebrant, on hearing your vows, simply proclaims you, now and *already*, 'man and wife'.

So what about the timeless, the eternal, and where does God come in? At the marriage service and beyond, God is your chief guest and principal witness. By inviting God to bless and sustain your vows, you are invoking your innermost self. The marriage vows are yours, and if you break them the responsibility will be yours alone. You cannot escape them by saying to yourself that you don't any longer reckon much to God, when the fact will be that you've broken faith with yourself, with the God within you. The marriage vows express your purpose, and as Hannah Whitall Smith puts it in *The Christian's Secret of a Happy Life*:

> It is your purpose God looks at, not your feelings about that purpose; and your purpose, or will, is therefore the only thing you need to attend to ... Let your emotions come or let them go, just as God pleases, and make no account of them either way ... They are not the indicators of your spiritual state, but are merely the indicators of your temperament or of your present physical condition.

Marriage has been held in common by societies all over the world well before the Christian Church was founded. Here's one instance described by Margaret Mead in her *Sex and Temperament in Three Primitive Societies*:

> . . . the girl makes herself a lovely grass skirt; with young wives a little older than she is, she spends many hours plaiting the sago-shoot shreds that she has wheedled some old woman into dyeing a beautiful red. She keeps her skin bathed and shining, and wears her necklace of opossum-teeth or dog's teeth every day. No one is fairer or gayer in the whole of Arapesh than these young girls waiting, in lovely attire, for life at last to catch up with them. No definite day is set; as the months pass, the parents relax their chaperonage more and more. The girl is fully matured now. The boy is tall and well developed. Some day the two, who are now allowed to go about alone together in the bush, will consummate their marriage, without haste, without a due date to harry them with its inevitableness, with no one to know or to comment, in response to a situation in which they have lived comfortably for years in the knowledge that they belong to each other.

The Christian Church's marriage service strongly implies that without God the creator, and without Jesus's example at a wedding in Cana of Galilee, marriage might be a lesser matter. It also proposes that marriage signifies the mystical union between Christ and his Church. That said, the Church goes on to confirm that marriage is made by the exchange of vows by the couple. The Liturgical Commission of the Church of England is considering the possibility of allowing divorcees who want to marry again to use the marriage service, and the provision of one rite to cover both church weddings and church 'blessings' after a civil marriage. It is also considering prayers of thanksgiving and direction for engaged couples when they first approach a priest about getting married. Dr Stancliffe, Bishop of Salisbury, has said that the purpose is to 'bring couples face to face with what they are taking on. Many couples are still at the stage of self-centred affection, and need help in setting the relationship in a broader context.'

> I have always felt that if you have made a commitment to someone, then marriage is the perfect way to cement that commitment. We are going to be married in the church in the village where we live in Hertfordshire.
>
> I love the idea of Hal and me walking into the church and making a solemn oath in front of all our friends and family, in the name of something that is much greater than all of us. Since I moved there six years ago, I have heard the church bells ringing every Sunday and I always wondered if, one day, they would ring for me. Now they will.
>
> Kim Wilde, in the *Daily Mail*, 17 August 1996

We now try, as lay people, to focus upon what we find to be the essential words of the marriage service. These are taken from the Church of England's *Alternative Service Book*.

The Introduction

> God is love, and those who live in love live in God: and God lives in them. (1 John 4:16)

> God our Father,
> You have taught us through your Son
> that love is the fulfilling of the law.

> Grant to your servants
> that, loving one another,
> they may continue in your love until their lives' end;
> through Jesus Christ our Lord.

The Marriage

> We have come together in the presence of God, to witness
> the marriage of *N* and *N*, to ask his blessing on them, and
> to share in their joy.

In other words, God is the chief guest at the wedding.

> The Scriptures teach us that marriage is a gift of God in
> creation and a means of his grace, a holy mystery in which
> man and woman become one flesh.

According to the Bible, in creating the world, God created Adam
and Eve to be husband and wife, and to produce children. This 'holy
mystery' emphasises the central place that marriage occupies in
society. The next paragraph from the marriage service expands upon
the meaning and purpose of marriage.

> Marriage is given, that husband and wife may comfort and
> help each other, living faithfully together in need and in
> plenty, in sorrow and in joy. It is given, that with delight
> and tenderness they may know each other in love, and,
> through the joy of their bodily union, may strengthen the
> union of their hearts and lives. It is given, that they may
> have children and be blessed in caring for them and
> bringing them up in accordance with God's will, to his
> praise and glory.

The reasons why marriage is 'given' include feelings, intentions
and actions. The marriage service acknowledges the possibility of
poverty and sorrow as well as of plenty and joy. It underlines that

marriage is for mutual comfort and help, and that it is a continuing process of getting to know each other in a togetherness strengthened by the act of love. Where there are children, the couple's first duty is to care for them.

> In marriage husband and wife belong to one another, and they begin a new life together in the community. It is a way of life that all should honour; and it must not be undertaken carelessly, lightly, or selfishly, but reverently, responsibly and after serious thought.

This statement emphasises that the couple's first loyalty is to each other and that together they are making a new start in the community, and that the community should have due regard for the married state. Furthermore, the state of marriage must be entered into responsibly and in a state of full awareness.

Now we come to the mutual intentions of the couple, in the form of the celebrant putting exactly the same question to the bridegroom and to the bride, to which each answers, 'I will'.

> *N*, will you take *N* to be your wife/husband? Will you love her/him, comfort her/him, honour and protect her/him, and, forsaking all others, be faithful to her/him as long as you both shall live?

Next follow the vows, the bridegroom and the bride clasping right hands. Each says:

> I, *N*, take you, *N*,
> to be my wife/husband,
> to have and to hold
> from this day forward;
> for better, for worse,
> for richer, for poorer,

in sickness and in health,
to love and to cherish,
till death us do part,
according to God's holy law;
and this is my solemn vow.

The service offers a choice of slightly different vows, where the bridegroom promises 'to love, cherish and worship', an echo of the words given in the *Book of Common Prayer*: 'With my body I thee worship.' The bride also has the choice of promising 'to love, cherish and obey', as expressed in the *Book of Common Prayer*.

Next comes the giving of the ring by the groom, or the exchange of rings between the couple:

I give you this ring
as a sign of our marriage.
With my body I honour you,
all that I am I give to you,
and all that I have I share with you,
within the love of God;
Father, Son and Holy Spirit.

When, earlier in this book, we urged that you should look into your hearts and examine your reasons for wishing to marry, these are the promises that we had most in mind. To honour your spouse with your body is not the same as taking your own satisfaction; it is a promise to give, not a readiness to receive. Also, in order to say 'all that I am I give to you', you must bring to that promise some degree of self-knowledge and self-awareness. So the exercise of examining yourself, your motives and your desires in wishing to get married is vital. Otherwise you are in danger of making this promise in ignorance. Also, 'all that I have I share with you' refers not only to money and possessions, but to personal qualities, hopes and fears.

The man and the woman have now married each other, and the celebrant proclaims:

> In the presence of God, and before this congregation, *N* and *N* have given their consent and made their marriage vows to each other. They have declared their marriage by the joining of hands and by the giving and receiving of a ring. I therefore proclaim that they are husband and wife.

Again, the couple clasp their right hands and the celebrant says:

> That which God has joined together,
> let not man divide.

This powerful edict (the *Book of Common Prayer* says, 'let no man put asunder') is often thought to point solely to divorce. We understand it to have a larger meaning. The married couple may encounter individuals in the community who have scant respect for marriage and who may even seek to undermine it. For example, a selfish employer may make insupportable demands in terms of hours worked or travel away from home; business colleagues, usually male, may scoff at marriage and encourage infidelity. There is also the vain and selfish seducer, man or woman, who may alienate the married person's affections and so strike at the foundations of the couple's relationship.

The Roman Catholic marriage service is similar to those of the Church of England and other Protestant Churches. It puts more emphasis on marital fidelity; the bride is not asked to promise to obey. The vows exchanged by the couple are virtually identical to those in the Church of England service. God's 'ordinance' for 'the propagation of children' is more strongly emphasised, as is the family:

By this marriage our two families have been united. May all of us, and particularly the parents of *N* and *N*, increase in affection for one another, and find in one another a source of help and strength.

The Roman Catholic service stresses the significance of marriage to and within the community. The priest may say this prayer:

May all married people here with us be reminded of the joy of their own wedding day. May they give thanks for all the happiness they have known. May each day find them ever more devoted to one another.

At the close of the service, the priest may say this blessing:

May you always bear witness to the love of God in the world so that the afflicted and needy will find in you generous friends, and welcome you into the joys of Heaven.

The Society of Friends (Quaker) wedding is simplicity itself. The bride and groom exchange vows of lifelong love and loyalty, and while a ring does not form a necessary part of the marriage – since the groom's word is considered his bond – the bride often receives a ring at the end of the ceremony. A reception afterwards is not encouraged, a tradition which seems to have been endorsed by Goethe, who writes:

One should only celebrate a happy ending; celebrations at the outset exhaust the joy and energy needed to urge us forward and sustain us in the long struggle. And of all celebrations a wedding is the worst; no day should be kept more quietly and humbly.

The spirit of Quaker marriage is well expressed in the following letter written by Job Scott to his betrothed in 1780 shortly before they wed:

> May we, the remainder of our lives, earnestly press after resignation to the Lord's will, and above all things, strive to please him who only can give peace, in whatever circumstances we may be. Then, I trust, the guardian angel of his holy presence will encamp around us, and his everlasting arms be underneath to support us.

Jewish communities have evolved in many different parts of the world, and the Jewish wedding may vary in custom as well as in the degree of orthodoxy. Jewish weddings place a strong emphasis on the significance of marriage for the community. The ceremony – which is rich in symbolism and punctuated by joyful psalms – celebrates marriage as the ideal human state, where the man, with the woman, perpetuates divine creation. It need not take place in a synagogue, but is always performed under a canopy – the *chuppah* – where the couple's parents stand and under which blessings are recited. The exchange of vows is similar to those of the Christian Churches. Then the groom places a ring on the forefinger of the bride's right hand and recites in Hebrew 'Behold, you are consecrated unto me by this ring, according to the law of Moses and of Israel.' This signifies positive action by the groom and acceptance by the bride. The bride and groom drink wine from a goblet. In many communities, once the ceremony is concluded, a glass is crushed underfoot by the groom and those present cry *Mazzeltov!* meaning 'Good luck and congratulations!'

Victor Gollancz, publisher, wrote in his autobiographical letter to his grandson, *My Dear Timothy*, the following account of his daughter's wedding which he blessed according to the Jewish tradition in which he himself had married:

I have always been glad I was married in synagogue (and I will add, for the sheer pleasure of recalling it, the total irrelevancy that your grandmother . . . looked indescribably beautiful in cloth of gold with white lilies). So I thought it a good idea that your mother should be married in one too, and she agreed with me. But the Rabbi of the synagogue to which I still nominally belonged had a scruple about marrying them there unless your father went in first for some Jewish instruction, which might have taken quite a long time; for he is only half-Jewish by birth. This suited no one: they wanted to be married at once, so that they could have you sooner. They were married, accordingly, by registrar; but when we got home I became a temporary Rabbi myself, for I had the temerity to marry them all over again before the assembled company, in accordance with the beautiful old ritual: blessings (in Hebrew, with English translations for the *goyim*) and canopy and wine-glass breaking and all.

The register office wedding, the civil ceremony, is in effect a legal marriage that has no religious significance. Just as a couple who are to be married in church must see the celebrant clergyman before the wedding for legal as well as for religious reasons, so they must pay a visit for legal reasons to the superintendent registrar at the office where they are to be married. The law requires only two witnesses to be present, and they will sign the register after the marriage.

I had vaguely supposed that marriage in a registry office while lacking both sanctity and style, was at least a swift, straightforward business. If not, then what was the use of it, even to the heathens? A few enquiries, however, showed it to be no such thing.

RICHARD ADAMS, *The Girl in a Swing*

The words read by the registrar at the ceremony, while containing no reference to God, express sentiments similar to those in the church service: that marriage is not to be entered into lightly; that the couple must not know of any reason why they are not free to marry; and that they pledge themselves to each other. The vows, while making no reference to 'in sickness and in health' or to their enduring 'till death us do part', are just as binding as those exchanged in church. Rings may be exchanged, though without religious significance.

Many people, even those who have no religious upbringing or belief, feel that the civil ceremony is somewhat bleak and perfunctory. It is much shorter than the church service, and there will not be room in the register office for more than thirty or forty people to be present, if that. Hence the provision of the 1994 Marriage Act which allows the civil wedding ceremony to take place in 'officially approved places' such as stately homes and hotels.

The wording of the marriage vows for all marriages taking place in England and Wales is legally prescribed by the 1994 Marriage Act, except for the Anglican Church, the Jewish communities and the Society of Friends (Quakers). The 1996 Marriage Ceremony (Prescribed Words) Act, which came into force on 1 February 1997, has put forward a new and optional form of words for civil marriages and non-Anglican religious denominations whose use will make the marriage ceremony shorter and simpler. The law in Scotland affords much greater freedom of choice where a religious wedding is concerned, but in contrast it regulates civil ceremonies more tightly.

A service of blessing may take place when a couple have been unable to marry in church. This may be because one or both have been divorced or they are from different religious traditions. The service would take place after the civil ceremony, and need not include marriage vows or other formalities. The celebrant gives a short address, and prayers are said to bless the marriage.

At this point it may be interesting to take a look at the history of the institution of marriage as it has evolved, particularly in England and Wales.

Until emancipation, the woman was required to make an absolute surrender to her husband of her liberty, her wealth and her possessions. Olwen Hufton in *The Prospect before Her: A History of Women in Western Europe* (Vol. 1, 1500–1800), reflects this in her account of Christian marriage in the sixteenth and seventeenth centuries:

> The model of the Christian marriage in the truly godly society is conceptualized [in *A Godly Form of Householde Government*, a popular manual at the time] as a patriarchal power relationship in which the husband must constantly invigilate his wife's conduct and bring her to account, but he must do so in a kindly way. Tyranny is not the intent. The relationship should be one of harmony in which the male and female complement each other. He creates wealth, she saves; he seeks a living, she keeps house; he deals openly with the world, she keeps herself apart from all but a few; his virtue is enhanced by skill in discourse, hers by silence. While he may give, she must save; while he can apparently bedeck himself at will provided he wears the trousers, she is urged to be discreet in dress. He is accountable in the next world to God; she is accountable in the here and now to her husband. Above all, while he negotiates the household's external relationships, the orderliness of the inner household is her preserve.

The seventeenth and eighteenth centuries saw a continuing effort to regulate the legalities of marriage in a society which placed growing importance upon birthright, property and the rights of inheritance, and which became increasingly concerned for the children of dubious marriages. There was much legal confusion as to the status of marriage. Many marriages were 'common law', with no religious or legal sanction; others were 'clandestine' marriages, performed by a priest of a sort, but without the banns being published; and others were conducted according to a religious framework in church. Many weddings still took place outside church, and the Churches campaigned to put the church ceremony at the heart of marriage as opposed to the custom of unsanctified ritual celebrations.

Between 1666 and 1718 no fewer than ten bills seeking to regulate and streamline the marriage ceremony were introduced in Parliament, until the state stepped in and formulated the rules that still basically obtain in England and Wales today, rules which stem from the terms of Hardwicke's Marriage Act of 1753. From then on marriage had to be not only a public matter but one requiring the sanction of the state, and so became an institution fundamental to society and public life, whereas before it had been essentially a private affair. The wedding as we know it reflects this history. The state (Anglican) Church and certain other Churches are empowered to ratify marriage according to the law as well as to celebrate it in the eyes of God. The wedding reception and partying before and after the wedding are a continuation of the private and community celebrations which marked marriage in earlier times.

Prayers

As well as the following prayers and pledges that may be made by or on behalf of bride and groom, many psalms or verses from them (see pages 51–8) may be said or sung as prayers. But first, last and always:

> Lord, thou knowest that we must be very busy this day.
> If we forget thee, yet do not thou forget us.
>
> ADAPTED FROM SIR JACOB ASTLEY

The Introduction

> God our Father, you have taught us through your Son that love is the fulfilling of the law. Grant to your servants that, loving one another, they may continue in your love until their lives end; through Jesus Christ our Lord.
>
> ALTERNATIVE SERVICE BOOK

God of love, we praise you.
You made the world in love, giving us freedom;
in Christ you lived by love, accepting all its hurt and
    sharing all its healing;
by your Spirit you are present in love, everywhere and
    always, here and now.
As we respond to your great love,

accept the worship and commitment we all bring,
and bless the commitment of N and N.
Let the love of Christ be present in everything done and
    begun today; through Jesus Christ our Lord.

Father, hear our prayers for N and N who, with faith in you
and in each other, pledge their love today. May they be as
aware of your presence as they are of ours, and confident
that you are able to help them fulfil their promises in their
life together; through Jesus Christ our Lord.

Living God, you have commanded us to love each other.
    We thank you now for the love which grows between a
man and a woman, which has brought these two together
here to declare themselves one before you and their
families and friends.
    As they make their promises to each other, may they do
so humbly and penitently [and in the confidence that you
will forgive all their failures of the past].
    May they begin their life together with your own love in
heart and mind, and may we all continue, all our lives, to
walk with you and glorify your name; through Jesus Christ
our Lord.

Patterns and Prayers for Christian Worship

The Bride's Pledge

My true love hath my heart, and I have his,
By just exchange one for the other given:
I hold his dear, and mine he cannot miss;
There never was a bargain better driven.
His heart in me keeps me and him in one;
My heart in him his thoughts and senses guides:

He loves my heart, for once it was his own;
I cherish his, because in me it bides.

SIR PHILIP SIDNEY

The Bride's Happiness

My heart is like a singing bird
  Whose nest is in a watered shoot;
My heart is like an apple-tree
  Whose boughs are bent with thickest fruit;
My heart is like a rainbow shell
  That paddles in a halcyon sea;
My heart is gladder than all these
  Because my love is come to me.

Raise me a dais of silk and down;
  Hang it with vair* and purple dyes;
Carve it in doves and pomegranates,
  And peacocks with a hundred eyes;
Work it in gold and silver grapes,
  In leaves and silver fleurs-de-lys;
Because the birthday of my life
  Is come, my love is come to me.

* vair = fur

CHRISTINA ROSSETTI

The Groom's Promise

I have loved you, oh mildest and fairest,
  With love that could scarce be more warm –
I have loved you, oh brightest and rarest,
  Not less for your mind than your form.
I've adored you since ever I met you,

O, Rose without briar or stain,
And if e'er I forsake or forget you
Let Love be ne'er trusted again.

TRANS. FROM THE Gaelic JAMES CLARENCE MANGAN

The Groom's Pledge

A heart as soft, a heart as kind,
    A heart as sound and free
As in the whole world thou canst find,
    That heart I'll give to thee.

Thou art my life, my love, my heart,
    The very eyes of me:
And hast command of every part
    To live and die for thee.

ROBERT HERRICK

The Gift of Love

The tides shall cease to beat the shore,
    The stars fall from the sky;
Yet I will love thee more and more
    Until the day I die, my dear,
    Until the day I die

ROBERT BURNS

Other Prayers

Almighty God,
you send your Holy Spirit
to be the life and light of all your people.
Open the hearts of these your children to the riches of his
    grace,
that they may bring forth the fruit of the Spirit

in love and joy and peace;
through Jesus Christ our Lord. Amen.

ALTERNATIVE SERVICE BOOK

Heavenly Father,
maker of all things,
you enable us to share in your work of creation.
Bless this couple in the gift and care of children,
that their home may be a place of love, security and truth,
and their children grow up to know and love you in your
    Son
Jesus Christ our Lord. Amen.

ALTERNATIVE SERVICE BOOK

Lord and Saviour Jesus Christ,
who shared at Nazareth the life of an earthly home:
reign in the home of these your servants as Lord and
    King;
give them grace to minister to others as you have
    ministered to men,
and grant that by deed and word
they may be witnesses of your saving love
to those among whom they live;
for the sake of your holy name. Amen.

ALTERNATIVE SERVICE BOOK

O God of Abraham, God of Isaac, God of Jacob, bless these
thy servants and sow the seed of eternal life in their hearts:
that whatsoever in thy holy Word they shall profitably learn,
they may in deed fulfil the same. Look, O Lord, mercifully
upon them from heaven, and bless them. And as thou didst
send thy blessing upon Abraham and Sarah, to their great
comfort, so vouchsafe to send thy blessing upon these thy
servants: that they obeying thy will, and alway being in

safety under thy protection, may abide in thy love unto their lives' end; through Jesus Christ our Lord. Amen.

BOOK OF COMMON PRAYER

Almighty God, who at the beginning did create our first parents, Adam and Eve, and did sanctify and join them together in marriage; Pour upon you the riches of his grace, sanctify and bless you, that ye may please him both in body and soul, and live together in holy love unto your lives' end. Amen.

BOOK OF COMMON PRAYER

Eternal God, Creator and Father of us all, we praise you for creating humanity male and female, so that each may find fulfilment in the other.

We praise you for the ways in which love comes into our lives, and for all the joys that can come to men and women through marriage.

Today, we thank you for N and N, for your gift to them of life, and for bringing them together in marriage.

We thank you for the love and care of their parents, which has guided them to maturity and prepared them for each other. We thank you for their commitment to one another and to a life planted in love and built on love. With them we pray for their parents, that at this moment of parting they may find new happiness as they share their children's joy.

Help N and N to keep the promises they have made, to be loyal and faithful to each other, and to support one another throughout their life together; may they bear each other's burdens and share each other's joys.

Help them to be honest and patient with each other, to be loving and wise parents of any children they have, and to make their home a place of welcome and peace.

In their future together, may they enjoy each other's lives and grow through each other's love; through Jesus Christ our Lord.

PATTERNS AND PRAYERS FOR CHRISTIAN WORSHIP

Our Father in heaven,
hallowed be your name,
your kingdom come,
your will be done,
on earth as in heaven.
Give us today our daily bread.
Forgive us our sins
as we forgive those who sin against us.
Lead us not into temptation
but deliver us from evil.
For the kingdom, the power, and the glory are yours
now and for ever. Amen.

ALTERNATIVE SERVICE BOOK

Our Father, which art in heaven, Hallowed be thy Name. Thy kingdom come. Thy will be done, in earth as it is in heaven. Give us this day our daily bread. And forgive us our trespasses, As we forgive them that trespass against us. And lead us not into temptation; But deliver us from evil: For thine is the kingdom, The power, and the glory, For ever and ever.

BOOK OF COMMON PRAYER

Dear God, may we look backward with gratitude, forward with courage, upwards with confidence.

ANON.

O God, give us the serenity to accept the things we cannot change; the courage to change the things we can; and the wisdom to know the difference.

ADAPTED FROM REINHOLD NIEBUHR

Give us, O Lord, a steadfast heart, which no unworthy affection may drag downwards; give us an unconquered heart, which no tribulation can wear out; give us an upright heart, which no unworthy purpose may tempt aside. Bestow upon us also, O Lord our God, understanding to know thee, diligence to seek thee, wisdom to find thee, and a faithfulness that may finally embrace thee; through Jesus Christ our Lord.

THOMAS AQUINAS

God of all goodness, grant us to desire ardently, to seek wisely, to know surely, and to accomplish perfectly thy holy will, for the glory of thy name.

THOMAS AQUINAS

O thou, from whom to be turned is to fall,
to whom to be turned is to rise,
and in whom to stand is to abide for ever;
grant us, in all our duties, thy help,
in all our perplexities, thy guidance,
in all our dangers, thy protection,
and in all our sorrows, thy peace;
through Jesus Christ our Lord.

ST AUGUSTINE OF HIPPO

Lord, make us instruments of thy peace.
  Where there is hatred let us sow love;
  Where there is injury, pardon;
  Where there is discord, union;

Where there is doubt, faith;
Where there is despair, hope;
Where there is darkness, light;
Where there is sadness, joy;

O Divine Master, grant that we may not so much seek to be consoled as to console; to be understood as to understand; to be loved, as to love; through the love of thy Son who died for us, Jesus Christ our Lord.

ST FRANCIS OF ASSISI

Remember, O Lord, what thou hast wrought in us, and not what we deserve; and, as thou hast called us to thy service, make us worthy of our calling; through Jesus Christ our Lord.

LEONINE SACRAMENTARY

O Lord, who has taught us that all our doings without charity are nothing worth: send thy Holy Ghost and pour into our hearts that most excellent gift of charity, the very bond of peace and of all virtues, without which whosoever liveth is counted dead before thee. Grant this for thine only Son Jesus Christ's sake.

ARCHBISHOP THOMAS CRANMER

O Lord God, when thou givest to thy servants to endeavour any great matter, grant us also to know that it is not the beginning but the continuing of the same unto the end, until it be thoroughly finished, which yieldeth the true glory; through him for the finishing of thy work laid down his Life, our Redeemer Jesus Christ.

SIR FRANCIS DRAKE

O God, our Father, help us all through this day so to live that we may bring help to others, credit to ourselves and to the name we bear, and joy to those that love us, and to you.

Cheerful when things go wrong;
Persevering when things are difficult;
Serene when things are irritating.
Enable us to be:
Helpful to those in difficulties;
Kind to those in need;
Sympathetic to those whose hearts are sore and sad.
Grant that:
Nothing may make us lose our tempers;
Nothing may take away our joy;
Nothing may ruffle our peace;
Nothing may make us bitter towards anyone.
So grant that through all this day all with whom we work,
and all those whom we meet, may see in us the reflection
of the master, whose we are, and whom we seek to serve.
This we ask for your love's sake.

WILLIAM BARCLAY

Almighty God, giver of life and love, bless N and N, whom
you have now joined in Christian marriage. Grant them
wisdom and devotion in their life together, that each may
be to the other a strength in need, a comfort in sorrow, and
a companion in joy. So unite their wills in your will, and
their spirits in your Spirit, that they live and grow together
in love and peace all the days of their life; through Jesus
Christ our Lord. Amen.

ALTERNATIVE SERVICE BOOK

Eternal God, true and loving Father, in holy marriage you
make your servants one. May their life together witness to
your love in this troubled world; may unity overcome
division, forgiveness heal injury, and joy triumph over
sorrow; through Jesus Christ our Lord. Amen.

ALTERNATIVE SERVICE BOOK

Heavenly Father,
we thank you that in our earthly lives
you speak to us of your eternal life:
we pray that through their marriage
N and N
may know you more clearly,
love you more dearly,
and follow you more nearly,
day by day;
through Jesus Christ our Lord. Amen.

ALTERNATIVE SERVICE BOOK

O God of love, look mercifully upon N and N in the new life which they begin together this day. Unite them evermore in your love. Keep them faithful to the vows they have made one to the other. Strengthen them with every good gift. And let your peace be with them, now and always; for the sake of Jesus Christ our Lord. Amen.

ALTERNATIVE SERVICE BOOK

O God, forasmuch as without thee we are not able to please thee; Mercifully grant, that thy Holy Spirit may in all things direct and rule our hearts; through Jesus Christ our Lord.

BOOK OF COMMON PRAYER

Almighty and everlasting God, mercifully look upon our infirmities, and in all our dangers and necessities stretch forth thy right hand to help and defend us; through Jesus Christ our Lord.

BOOK OF COMMON PRAYER

Almighty God, who seest that we have no power of ourselves to help ourselves; Keep us both outwardly in our bodies, and inwardly in our souls; that we may be defended from all adversities which may happen to the body, and from all evil thoughts which may assault and hurt the soul; through Jesus Christ our Lord.

BOOK OF COMMON PRAYER

Almighty and everlasting God, who art always more ready to hear than we to pray, and art wont to give more than either we desire or deserve; Pour down upon us the abundance of thy mercy; forgiving us those things whereof our conscience is afraid, and giving us those good things which we are not worthy to ask, but through the merits and mediation of Jesus Christ, thy Son, our Lord.

BOOK OF COMMON PRAYER

O Almighty God, who hast knit together thine elect in one communion and fellowship, in the mystical body of thy Son Christ our Lord; Grant us grace so to follow thy blessed Saints in all virtuous and godly living, that we may come to those unspeakable joys, which thou hast prepared for them that unfeignedly love thee; through Jesus Christ our Lord.

BOOK OF COMMON PRAYER

Almighty God, Father of all mercies, we thine unworthy servants do give thee most humble and hearty thanks for all thy goodness and loving-kindness to us, and to all men; We bless thee for our creation, preservation, and all the blessings of this life; but above all, for thine inestimable love in the redemption of the world by our Lord Jesus Christ; for the means of grace and for the hope of glory. And, we beseech thee, give us that due sense of all thy mercies, that our hearts may be unfeignedly thankful, and that we shew forth thy praise, not only with our lips, but in our lives; by giving up ourselves to thy service, and by walking before thee in holiness and righteousness all our days; through Jesus Christ our Lord, to whom with thee and the Holy Ghost be all honour and glory, world without end.

Book of Common Prayer

Dear Lord and Father of mankind,
we thank you for the ordinance of marriage
by which man and woman find fulfilment
in their love for one another.
Bless all Christian husbands and wives.
May your presence enrich their love
and direct their way in life;
and keep them close to each other
in both good times and bad;
through Jesus Christ our Lord.

ADAPTED BY Frank Colquhoun

Almighty God and Father, we thank you that you have created us male and female in your own image, to share in your divine life and to fulfil our high destiny in marriage.

Help us to recognise the sanctity of the marriage bond, and to see in the love of man and woman a mirror of your everlasting love; through Jesus Christ our Lord.

Frank Colquhoun

God be in my head, and in my understanding;
God be in mine eyes, and in my looking;
God be in my mouth, and in my speaking;
God be in my heart, and in my thinking;
God be at mine end, and at my departing.

Sarum Prayer

Blessings

God the Holy Trinity make you strong in faith and love, defend you on every side, and guide you in truth and peace; and the blessing of God almighty, the Father, the Son, and the Holy Spirit, be among you and remain with you always. Amen.

ALTERNATIVE SERVICE BOOK

O Eternal God, Creator and Preserver of all mankind, Giver of all spiritual grace, the Author of everlasting life; Send thy blessing upon these thy servants, this man and this woman, whom we bless in thy Name; that, as Isaac and Rebecca lived faithfully together, so these persons may surely perform and keep the vow and covenant betwixt them made, (whereof this Ring given and received is a token and pledge), and may ever remain in perfect love and peace together, and live according to thy laws: through Jesus Christ our Lord.

BOOK OF COMMON PRAYER

Grant, O Lord, that we may walk in your presence, with your love in our hearts, your trust in our minds, your strength in our wills: that when we finally stand before you, it may be with the assurance of your welcome and the joy of our homecoming. And the blessing of God Almighty, the Father, the Son and the Holy Spirit rest upon you and be with you, now and always.

Deep peace of the running wave to you
Deep peace of the flowing air to you
Deep peace of the quiet earth to you
Deep peace of the shining stars to you
Deep peace of the Son of peace to you.

IONA COMMUNITY PRAYER

The Lord bless you and keep you; the Lord make his face shine upon you and be gracious to you; the Lord turn his face towards you and give you peace.

NUMBERS 6:24–6

Go happy youth, at length the day is come
That thou shalt claim thine own, the much lov'd one;
Oh! May that love be never known to cease,
But ever, ever, with thy years increase.

She leaves her mother's home to be thy Bride,
Then may she always in thy love confide;
Passing through life, so as that love to claim,
And e'en to death thy confidence retain.

Oh! May God bless you both, and may you shew
Your love to Him while sojourning below,
By ever helping such as are distressed
And, rest assured, your efforts will be blest.

WRITTEN ON THE OCCASION OF THOMAS WEST PORTER'S
MARRIAGE TO MARY JANE WAINE BY HIS MOTHER, 1871

Psalms

The following psalms are taken from the Book of Common Prayer by permission (see page 254–60).

The heavens declare the glory of God: and the firmament sheweth his handywork.

One day telleth another: and one night certifieth another.

There is neither speech nor language: but their voices are heard among them.

Their sound is gone out into all lands: and their words into the ends of the world.

In them hath he set a tabernacle for the sun: which cometh forth as a bridegroom out of his chamber, and rejoiceth as a giant to run his course.

It goeth forth from the uttermost part of the heaven, and runneth about unto the end of it again: and there is nothing hid from the heat thereof.

Let the words of my mouth, and the meditation of my heart: be alway acceptable in thy sight.

O Lord: my strength, and my redeemer.

PSALM 19:1–6, 14–15

The Lord is my shepherd: therefore can I lack nothing.

He shall feed me in a green pasture: and lead me forth beside the waters of comfort.

He shall convert my soul: and bring me forth in the paths
of righteousness, for his Name's sake.

Yea, though I walk through the valley of the shadow of
death, I will fear no evil: for thou art with me; thy rod and
thy staff comfort me.

Thou shalt prepare a table before me against them that
trouble me: thou hast anointed my head with oil, and my cup
shall be full.

But thy loving-kindness and mercy shall follow me all the
days of my life: and I will dwell in the house of the Lord for
ever.

Psalm 23

My heart is inditing of a good matter: I speak of the things
which I have made unto the King.

My tongue is the pen: of a ready writer.

Thou art fairer than the children of men: full of grace are
thy lips, because God hath blessed thee for ever.

Thou hast loved righteousness, and hated iniquity: where-
fore God, even thy God, hath anointed thee with the oil of
gladness above thy fellows.

All thy garments smell of myrrh, aloes and cassia: out of
ivory palaces, whereby they have made thee glad.

King's daughters were among thy honourable women: upon
thy right hand did stand the queen in a vesture of gold,
wrought about with divers colours.

Hearken, O daughter, and consider, incline thine ear:
forget also thine own people, and thy father's house.

So shall the King have pleasure in thy beauty: for he is thy
Lord God, and worship thou him.

And the daughter of Tyre shall be there with a gift: like as
the rich also among the people shall make their supplication
before thee.

The King's daughter is all glorious within: her clothing is
of wrought gold.

She shall be brought unto the King in raiment of
needlework: the virgins that be her fellows shall bear her
company, and shall be brought unto thee.

With joy and gladness shall they be brought: and shall
enter into the King's palace.

Instead of thy fathers thou shalt have children: whom thou
mayest make princes in all lands.

I will remember thy name from one generation to another:
therefore shall the people give thanks unto thee, world
without end.

PSALM 45:1–3, 8–18

God be merciful unto us, and bless us: and shew us the light
of his countenance, and be merciful unto us;

That thy way may be known upon earth: thy saving health
among all nations.

Let the people praise thee, O God: yea, let all the people
praise thee.

O let the nations rejoice and be glad: for thou shalt judge
the folk righteously, and govern the nations upon earth.

Let the people praise thee, O God: let all the people praise
thee.

Then shall the earth bring forth her increase: and God,
even our own God, shall give us his blessing.

God shall bless us: and all the ends of the world shall fear
him.

PSALM 67

O how amiable are thy dwellings: thou Lord of hosts!

My soul hath a desire and longing to enter into the courts
of the Lord: my heart and my flesh rejoice in the living God.

Yea, the sparrow hath found her an house, and the swallow a nest where she may lay her young: even thy altars, O Lord of hosts, my King and my God.

Blessed are they that dwell in thy house: they will be alway praising thee.

Blessed is the man whose strength is in thee: in whose heart are thy ways.

Who going through the vale of misery use it for a well: and the pools are filled with water.

They will go from strength to strength: and unto the God of gods appeareth every one of them in Sion.

O Lord God of hosts, hear my prayer: hearken, O God of Jacob.

Behold, O God our defender: and look upon the face of thine Anointed.

For one day in thy courts: is better than a thousand.

I had rather be a door-keeper in the house of my God: than to dwell in the tents of ungodliness.

For the Lord God is a light and defence: the Lord will give grace and worship, and no good thing shall he withhold from them that live a godly life.

O Lord God of hosts: blessed is the man that putteth his trust in thee.

PSALM 84

My song shall be of mercy and judgement: unto thee, O Lord, will I sing.

O let me have understanding: in the way of godliness.

When wilt thou come unto me: I will walk in my house with a perfect heart.

I will take no wicked thing in hand; I hate the sins of unfaithfulness: there shall no such cleave unto me.

A froward heart shall depart from me: I will not know a wicked person.

Whoso privily slandereth his neighbour: him will I destroy.

Whoso hath also a proud look and high stomach: I will not suffer him.

Mine eyes look upon such as are faithful in the land: that they may dwell with me.

Whoso leadeth a godly life: he shall be my servant.

There shall no deceitful person dwell in my house: he that telleth lies shall not tarry in my sight.

PSALM 101:1–10

Praise the Lord, O my soul: O Lord my God, thou art become exceeding glorious; thou art clothed with majesty and honour.

Thou deckest thyself with light as it were with a garment: and spreadest out the heavens like a curtain.

Who layeth the beams of his chambers in the waters: and maketh the clouds his chariot, and walketh upon the wings of the wind.

He sendeth the springs into the rivers: which run among the hills.

All beasts of the field drink thereof: and the wild asses quench their thirst.

Beside them shall the fowls of the air have their habitation: and sing among the branches.

He watereth the hills from above: the earth is filled with the fruit of thy works.

He bringeth forth grass for the cattle: and green herb for the service of men.

That he may bring food out of the earth, and wine that maketh glad the heart of man: and oil to make him a cheerful countenance, and bread to strengthen man's heart.

The trees of the Lord also are full of sap: even the cedars of Libanus which he hath planted;

Wherein the birds make their nests: and the fir-trees are a dwelling for the stork.

The high hills are a refuge for the wild goats: and so are the stony rocks for the conies.

He appointed the moon for certain seasons: and the sun knoweth his going down.

Man goeth forth to his work, and to his labour: until the evening.

O Lord, how manifold are thy works: in wisdom hast thou made them all; the earth is full of thy riches.

I will sing unto the Lord as long as I live: I will praise my God while I have my being.

And so shall my words please him: my joy shall be in the Lord.

PSALM 104:1–3, 10–19, 23–4, 33–4

O God, my heart is ready, my heart is ready: I will sing and give praise with the best member that I have.

Awake, thou lute, and harp: I myself will awake right early.

I will give thanks unto thee, O Lord, among the people: I will sing praises unto thee among the nations.

For thy mercy is greater than the heavens: and thy truth reacheth unto the clouds.

Set up thyself, O God, above the heavens: and thy glory above all the earth.

That thy beloved may be delivered: let thy right hand save them, and hear thou me.

PSALM 108:1–6

I will lift up mine eyes unto the hills: from whence cometh my help.

My help cometh even from the Lord: who hath made heaven and earth.

He will not suffer thy foot to be moved: and he that keepeth thee will not sleep.

Behold, he that keepeth Israel: shall neither slumber nor sleep.

The Lord himself is thy keeper: the Lord is thy defence upon thy right hand.

So that the sun shall not burn thee by day: neither the moon by night.

The Lord shall preserve thee from all evil: yea, it is even he that shall keep thy soul.

The Lord shall preserve thy going out, and thy coming in: from this time forth for evermore.

PSALM 121

Blessed are all they that fear the Lord: and walk in his ways.

For thou shalt eat the labours of thine hands: O well is thee, and happy shalt thou be.

Thy wife shall be as the fruitful vine: upon the walls of thine house.

Thy children like the olive-branches: round about thy table.

Lo, thus shall the man be blessed: that feareth the Lord.

The Lord from out of Sion shall so bless thee: that thou shalt see Jerusalem in prosperity all thy life long.

Yea, that thou shalt see thy children's children: and peace upon Israel.

PSALM 128

O praise God in his holiness: praise him in the firmament of his power.

Praise him in his noble acts: praise him according to his excellent greatness.

Praise him in the sound of the trumpet: praise him upon the lute and harp.

Praise him in the cymbals and dances: praise him upon the strings and pipe.

Praise him upon the well-tuned cymbals: praise him upon the loud cymbals.

Let every thing that hath breath: praise the Lord.

PSALM 150

The Word

The following passages from the Holy Bible are taken from the Authorised Version of the Bible (the King James Bible) and from the Holy Bible, New International Version, by permission (see page 254–60). The source of each passage is indicated AV and NIV respectively.

Creation

Then God said, 'Let us make human beings in our image, in our likeness, and let them rule over the fish of the sea and the birds of the air, over the livestock, over all the earth, and over all the creatures that move along the ground.'

So God created human beings in his own image, in the image of God he created them; male and female he created them.

God blessed them and said to them, 'Be fruitful and increase in number; fill the earth and subdue it. Rule over the fish of the sea and the birds of the air and over every living creature that moves on the ground.'

Then God said, 'I give you every seed-bearing plant on the face of the whole earth and every tree that has fruit with seed in it. They will be yours for food. And to all the beasts of the earth and all the birds of the air and all the creatures that move on the ground – everything that has the breath of life in it – I give every green plant for food.' And it was so.

God saw all that he had made, and it was very good. And there was evening, and there was morning – the sixth day.

GENESIS 1:26–31 (NIV)

Husband and Wife

The Lord God said, 'It is not good for the man to be alone. I will make a helper suitable for him.'

Now the Lord God had formed out of the ground all the beasts of the field and all the birds of the air. He brought them to the man to see what he would name them; and whatever the man called each living creature, that was its name. So the man gave names to all the livestock, the birds of the air and all the beasts of the field.

But for Adam no suitable helper was found. So the Lord God caused the man to fall into a deep sleep; and while he was sleeping, he took one of the man's ribs and closed up the place with flesh. Then the Lord God made a woman from the rib he had taken out of the man, and he brought her to the man.

The man said, 'This is now bone of my bones and flesh of my flesh; she shall be called "woman", for she was taken out of man.'

For this reason a man will leave his father and mother and be united to his wife, and they will become one flesh.

GENESIS 2:18–24 (NIV)

A Virtuous Woman

Who can find a virtuous woman? for her price is far above rubies.

The heart of her husband doth safely trust in her, so that he shall have no need of spoil.

She will do him good and not evil all the days of her life.

She seeketh wool, and flax, and worketh willingly with her hands.

She is like the merchants' ships; she bringeth her food from afar.

She riseth also while it is yet night, and giveth meat to her household, and a portion to her maidens.

She considereth a field, and buyeth it: with the fruit of her hands she planteth a vineyard.

She girdeth her loins with strength, and strengtheneth her arms.

She perceiveth that her merchandise is good: her candle goeth not out by night.

She layeth her hands to the spindle, and her hands hold the distaff.

She stretcheth out her hand to the poor; yea, she reacheth forth her hands to the needy.

She is not afraid of the snow for her household: for all her household are clothed with scarlet.

She maketh herself coverings of tapestry; her clothing is silk and purple.

Her husband is known in the gates, when he sitteth among the elders of the land.

She maketh fine linen, and selleth it; and delivereth girdles unto the merchant.

Strength and honour are her clothing; and she shall rejoice in time to come.

She openeth her mouth with wisdom; and in her tongue is the law of kindness.

She looketh well to the ways of her household, and eateth not the bread of idleness.

Her children arise up, and call her blessed; her husband also, and he praiseth her.

Many daughters have done virtuously, but thou excellest

them all.

Favour is deceitful, and beauty is vain: but a woman that feareth the Lord, she shall be praised.

Give her of the fruit of her hands; and let her own works praise her in the gates.

PROVERBS 31:10–31 (AV)

Two Are Better than One

Two are better than one; because they have a good reward for their labour.

For if they fall, the one will lift up his fellow: but woe to him that is alone when he falleth; for he hath not another to help him up.

Again, if two lie together, then they have heat: but how can one be warm alone?

ECCLESIASTES 4:9–11 (AV)

The Love of Christ

For this cause I bow my knees unto the Father of our Lord Jesus Christ,

Of whom the whole family in heaven and earth is named,

That he would grant you, according to the riches of his glory, to be strengthened with might by his Spirit in the inner man;

That Christ may dwell in your hearts by faith; that ye, being rooted and grounded in love,

May be able to comprehend with all saints what is the breadth, and length, and depth, and height;

And to know the love of Christ, which passeth knowledge, that ye might be filled with all the fulness of God.

Now unto him that is able to do exceeding abundantly above all that we ask or think, according to the power that worketh in us,

Unto him be glory in the church by Christ Jesus
throughout all ages, world without end. Amen.

EPHESIANS 3:14–21 (AV)

My Beloved

The voice of my beloved! behold, he cometh leaping upon the
mountains, skipping upon the hills.

My beloved is like a roe or a young hart: behold, he
standeth behind our wall, he looketh forth at the windows,
shewing himself through the lattice.

My beloved spake, and said unto me, Rise up, my love, my
fair one, and come away.

For lo, the winter is past, the rain is over and gone;

The flowers appear on the earth; the time of the singing of
birds is come, and the voice of the turtle is heard in our land;

The fig tree putteth forth her green figs, and the vines
with the tender grape give a good smell. Arise, my love, my
fair one, and come away.

O my dove, that art in the clefts of the rock, in the secret
places of the stairs, let me see thy countenance, let me hear
thy voice; for sweet is thy voice, and thy countenance is
comely.

Take us the foxes, the little foxes, that spoil the vines: for
our vines have tender grapes.

My beloved is mine, and I am his: he feedeth among the
lilies.

Until the day break, and the shadows flee away, turn, my
beloved, and be thou like a roe or a young hart upon the
mountains of Bether.

SONG OF SOLOMON 2:8–17 (AV)

Forgiving

Put on therefore, as the elect of God, holy and beloved,
bowels of mercies, kindness, humbleness of mind, meekness,
longsuffering;

Forbearing one another, and forgiving one another, if any
man have a quarrel against any: even as Christ forgave you,
so also do ye.

And above all these things put on charity, which is the
bond of perfectness.

And let the peace of God rule in your hearts, to the which
also ye are called in one body; and be ye thankful.

Let the word of Christ dwell in you richly in all wisdom;
teaching and admonishing one another in psalms and hymns
and spiritual songs, singing with grace in your hearts to the
Lord.

And whatsoever ye do in word or deed, do all in the name
of the Lord Jesus, giving thanks to God and the Father by
him.

Wives, submit yourselves unto your own husbands, as it is
fit in the Lord.

Husband, love your wives, and be not bitter against them.

COLOSSIANS 3:12–17 (AV)

Proverbs (NIV)

> May your fountain be blessed,
>   and may you rejoice in the wife of your youth.
> A loving doe, a graceful deer –
>   may her breasts satisfy you always,
>   may you ever be captivated by her love.

5:18–19

The Proverbs of Solomon

Hatred stirs up dissension,
    but love covers over all wrongs.   10:12

A kind-hearted woman gains respect,
    but ruthless men gain only wealth.   11:16

Reckless words pierce like a sword,
    but the tongue of the wise brings healing.   12:18

Truthful lips endure for ever,
    but a lying tongue lasts only a moment.   12:19

The wise woman builds her house,
    but with her own hands the foolish one tears hers down.
                    14:1

Even in laughter the heart may ache,
    and joy may end in grief.   14:13

A heart at peace gives life to the body,
    but envy rots the bones.   14:30

A gentle answer turns away wrath,
    but a harsh word stirs up anger.   15:1

The tongue that brings healing is a tree of life,
    but a deceitful tongue crushes the spirit.   15:4

A happy heart makes the face cheerful,
    but heartache crushes the spirit.   15:13

Better a meal of vegetables where there is love
    than a fattened calf with hatred.   15:17

A cheerful look brings joy to the heart,
    and good news gives health to the bones.   15:30

Pleasant words are a honeycomb,
    sweet to the soul and healing to the bones.   16:24

Better a dry crust with peace and quiet
    than a house full of feasting, with strife.   17:1

Children's children are a crown to the aged,
    and parents are the pride of their children.   17:6

Starting a quarrel is like breaching a dam;
    so drop the matter before a dispute breaks out.   17:14

A cheerful heart is good medicine,
    but a crushed spirit dries up the bones.   17:22

He who finds a wife finds what is good
    and receives favour from the Lord.   18:22

An honest answer
    is like a kiss on the lips.   24:26

A quarrelsome wife is like
    a constant dripping on a rainy day;
restraining her is like restraining the wind
    or grasping oil with the hand.   27:15–16

There are three things that are too amazing for me,
    four that I do not understand:
the way of an eagle in the sky,
    the way of a snake on a rock,
the way of a ship on the high seas,
    and the way of a man with a young woman.   30:18–19

Love

Place me like a seal over your heart,
    like a seal on your arm;
for love is as strong as death,
    its jealousy* unyielding as the grave.
It burns like blazing fire,
    like a mighty flame.
Many waters cannot quench love;

rivers cannot wash it away.
If one were to give
    all the wealth of his house for love,
    it** would be utterly scorned.

* ardour
** he

SONG OF SONGS 8:6–7 (NIV)

Come Away

I am a wall,
    and my breasts are like towers.
Thus I have become in his eyes
    like one bringing contentment.

Come away, my lover,
    and be like a gazelle
or like a young stag
    on the spice-laden mountains.

SONG OF SONGS 8:10, 14 (NIV)

Water into Wine

On the third day a wedding took place at Cana in Galilee. Jesus' mother was there, and Jesus and his disciples had also been invited to the wedding. When the wine was gone, Jesus' mother said to him, 'They have no more wine.'

'Dear woman, why do you involve me?' Jesus replied. 'My time has not yet come.'

His mother said to the servants, 'Do whatever he tells you.'

Nearby stood six stone water jars, the kind used by the Jews for ceremonial washing, each holding from twenty to thirty gallons.

Jesus said to the servants, 'Fill the jars with water'; so they filled them to the brim.

Then he told them, 'Now draw some out and take it to the master of the banquet.'

They did so, and the master of the banquet tasted the water that had been turned into wine. He did not realise where it had come from, though the servants who had drawn the water knew. Then he called the bridegroom aside and said, 'Everyone brings out the choice wine first and then the cheaper wine after the guests have had too much to drink; but you have saved the best till now.'

This, the first of his miraculous signs, Jesus performed at Cana in Galilee. He thus revealed his glory, and his disciples put their faith in him.

JOHN 2:1–11 (NIV)

Mutual Love

Submit to one another out of reverence for Christ.

Wives, submit to your husbands as to the Lord. For the husband is the head of the wife as Christ is the head of the church, his body, of which he is the Saviour. Now as the church submits to Christ, so also wives should submit to their husbands in everything.

Husbands, love your wives, just as Christ loved the church and gave himself up for her to make her holy, cleansing her by the washing with water through the word, and to present her to himself as a radiant church, without stain or wrinkle or any other blemish, but holy and blameless. In this same way, husbands ought to love their wives as their own bodies. He who loves his wife loves himself. After all, people have never hated their own bodies, but feed and care for them, just as Christ does the church – for we are members of his body. 'For this reason a man will

leave his father and mother and be united to his wife, and
the two will become one flesh.' This is a profound mystery
– but I am talking about Christ and the church. However,
each one of you also must love his wife as he loves himself,
and the wife must respect her husband.

EPHESIANS 5:21–33 (NIV)

Love One Another

I am the vine, ye are the branches: He that abideth in me,
and I in him, the same bringeth forth much fruit: for without me ye can do nothing.

If a man abide not in me, he is cast forth as a branch, and
is withered; and men gather them, and cast them into the
fire, and they are burned.

If ye abide in me, and my words abide in you, ye shall
ask what ye will, and it shall be done unto you.

Herein is my Father glorified, that ye bear much fruit; so
shall ye be my disciples.

As the Father hath loved me, so have I loved you: continue ye in my love.

If ye keep my commandments, ye shall abide in my love;
even as I have kept my Father's commandments, and abide
in his love.

These things have I spoken unto you, that my joy might
remain in you, and that your joy might be full.

This is my commandment, That ye love one another, as I
have loved you.

JOHN 15:5–12 (AV)

Wives and Husbands

Wives, in the same way be submissive to your husbands so that, if any of them do not believe the word, they may be won over without words by the behaviour of their wives, when they see the purity and reverence of your lives. Your beauty should not come from outward adornment, such as braided hair and the wearing of gold jewellery and fine clothes. Instead, it should be that of your inner self, the unfading beauty of a gentle and quiet spirit, which is of great worth in God's sight. For this is the way the holy women of the past who put their hope in God used to make themselves beautiful. They were submissive to their own husbands, like Sarah, who obeyed Abraham and called him her master. You are her daughters if you do what is right and do not give way to fear.

Husbands, in the same way be considerate as you live with your wives, and treat them with respect as the weaker partner and as heirs with you of the gracious gift of life, so that nothing will hinder your prayers.

1 Peter 3:1–7 (NIV)

Walk in Love

It has given me great joy to find some of your children walking in the truth, just as the Father commanded us. And now, dear lady, I am not writing you a new command but one we have had from the beginning. I ask that we love one another. And this is love: that we walk in obedience to his commands. As you have heard from the beginning, his command is that you walk in love.

2 John: 4–6 (NIV)

God Is Love

Beloved, let us love one another: for love is of God: and every one that loveth is born of God, and knoweth God.

He that loveth not knoweth not God; for God is love.

In this was manifested the love of God toward us, because that God sent his only begotten Son into the world, that we might live through him.

Herein is love, not that we loved God, but that he loved us, and sent his Son to be the propitiation for our sins.

Beloved, if God so loved us, we ought also to love one another.

No man hath seen God at any time. If we love one another, God dwelleth in us, and his love is perfected in us.

1 JOHN 4:7–12 (AV)

The Wedding of Sara and Tobias

Tobias said, I will eat nothing here, till we agree and swear one to another.

Raguel said, Then take her from henceforth according to the manner, for thou art her cousin, and she is thine, and the merciful God give you good success in all things.

Then he called his daughter Sara, and she came to her father, and he took her by the hand, and gave her to be wife to Tobias, saying, Behold, take her after the law of Moses, and lead her away to thy father. And he blessed them;

And called Edna his wife, and took paper, and did write an instrument *of covenants*, and sealed it.

Then they began to eat.

TOBIT 7:11–15, *Apocrypha* (AV)

The Grace of a Wife

The grace of a wife delighteth her husband, and her discretion will fatten his bones.

A silent and loving woman is a gift of the Lord; and there is nothing so much worth as a mind well instructed.

A shamefaced and faithful woman is a double grace, and her continent mind cannot be valued.

As the sun when it ariseth in the high heaven; so is the beauty of a good wife in the ordering of her house.

As the clear light is upon the holy candlestick; so is the beauty of the face in ripe age.

As the golden pillars are upon the sockets of silver; so are the fair feet with a constant heart.

My son, keep the flower of thine age sound; and give not thy strength to strangers.

When thou hast gotten a fruitful possession through all the field, sow it with thine own seed, trusting in the goodness of thy stock.

So thy race which thou leavest shall be magnified, having the confidence of their good descent.

An harlot shall be accounted as spittle; but a married woman is a tower against death to her husband.

A wicked woman is given as a portion to a wicked man: but a godly woman is given to him that feareth the Lord.

A dishonest woman contemneth shame: but an honest woman will reverence her husband.

A shameless woman shall be counted as a dog; but she that is shamefaced will fear the Lord.

A woman that honoureth her husband shall be judged wise of all; but she that dishonoureth him in her pride shall be counted ungodly of all.

ECCLESIASTICUS 26:13–26, *Apocrypha* (AV)

A Wife with her Husband

Bountifulness is as a most fruitful garden, and mercifulness endureth for ever.

To labour, and to be content with that a man hath, is a sweet life: but he that findeth a treasure is above them both.

Children and the building of a city continue a man's name: but a blameless wife is counted above them both.

Wine and musick rejoice the heart; but the love of wisdom is above them both.

The pipe and the psaltery make sweet melody: but a pleasant tongue is above them both.

Thine eye desireth favour and beauty: but more than both corn while it is green.

A friend and companion never meet amiss: but above both is a wife with her husband.

ECCLESIASTICUS 40:17–23, *Apocrypha* (AV)

Marriage

Why do we talk about a relationship *ending* in marriage? Shouldn't it *start* there?

QUOTED IN REGINA BARRECA, *PERFECT HUSBANDS*
(AND *OTHER FAIRY TALES*)

The newly-married couple has the faith and the hope that they will live happily ever after. If they didn't, they probably would not have taken the plunge. But the marriage can and often does discover the unexpected. The adjustment to being a couple, as opposed to individuals, may expose hitherto unacknowledged weaknesses and strengths. The person who, up to the wedding, has been compliant may be resistant when married; the person who has been indulgent towards the other may become stringent.

It is not just that the one may find the other's behaviour unfamiliar, even upsetting, and requiring adjustment on their part; it is that they may find their *own* reactions to situations – even everyday ones – within marriage surprising. One can be taken unawares by one's own responses, quite as much as by the reactions of one's spouse. This is why the business of self-examination as well as of getting to know, as far as possible, the one you love *before* marriage is so important. Then, to get married is not so much a plunge in the dark (there may be no water in the swimming pool), as of taking a dive with one's eyes open in the light of full awareness, even though one may not be able to discern everything that may lurk beneath the surface.

The unexpected continually knocks at the door of marriage: births, deaths, unforeseen opportunities, unlooked-for reverses. Marriage is there to absorb, sustain and cushion the unexpected. It is also a soil from which, when well cultivated, a mutuality of interests and affections may spring and grow.

The writer Naomi Jacob in *Me – Thinking Things Over* calls marriage 'one of the most difficult conditions imaginable':

> Two people living in close proximity, expected by convention to share interests, amusements, holidays, and the daily trivial annoyances which come to us all must sooner or later feel the strain of that perpetual companionship. Particularly if they marry when they are fairly young and are not completely developed. Their very mental development may be along completely different lines ... I have known, and probably so have you, ideally happy marriages and they were not those where husband and wife each went their own way, but where husband and wife wanted to go the same way, to enjoy the same things, found their interests more interesting because they were shared.

'Their very mental development may be along completely different lines.' This remark points to the unexpected: not to beware of it, but to be prepared for it. To succeed, marriage must allow room for the individual's growth as well as for the defence of the (often narrowly perceived) institution of marriage.

Arnold Bennett, in *Mental Efficiency*, had tough things to say:

> Personally, I should estimate that not in one per cent. even of romantic marriages are the husband and wife capable of *passion* for each other after three years. So brief is the violence of love! In perhaps thirty-three per cent. passion settles down into a tranquil affection – which is ideal. In fifty per cent. it sinks into sheer indifference, and one

becomes used to one's wife or one's husband as to one's other habits. And in the remaining sixteen per cent. it develops into dislike or detestation.

Clearly, these percentages are plucked out of the air and Bennett's approach is no more than quasi-scientific. Yet he represents a modern view of marriage which has been as widely held as it is pernicious. He refers to the 'violence' of love; but what of love's tenderness? Why should 'passion' not *deepen* into 'affection', still loving, and without the 'violence'? Bennett's estimation of marriage in the first part of the twentieth century may be broadly right, and his thought is sobering. But his pronouncement reeks of sterile rationality. He sees marriage as a 'closed system' (which it still can be) rather than as a stepping-out into the wider society and as a framework for the individual's further development.

That 'framework' is vital. If the individual steps outside it – into protracted periods of separation, into their own secret inner self, and/or into infidelity – the marriage is at risk. Separation can only be tolerated by a mature couple who have won through to a deep knowledge, love and understanding of one another; it's not for the passionate young, with or without young children. Nor can a hidden self, kept secret over time, where words and actions may utterly belie what is actually going on within the person's thoughts and feelings, be tolerated by a loving spouse, who will suffer increasing bafflement and hurt thereby. Infidelity may be forgiven, but the initial hurt to the one who has been betrayed is usually massive and leaves an indelible scar. Bertrand Russell, writing of his emancipated respect for his wife's liberty, found that his

> capacity for forgiveness and what may be called Christian love was not equal to the demands that I was making on it, and that persistence in a hopeless endeavour would do much harm to me, while not achieving the intended good to others . . . I was blinded by theory.

What Russell found by painful experience was that there are limits to tolerance, and he admits that the theory of total freedom within marriage, by ignoring those limits, was for him a recipe for disaster. Every couple should gently explore together where those limits lie for them, and should not marry until they have at least begun to understand each other's boundaries. These are by no means confined to infidelity. One person may indicate that they may depend, at least from time to time, on a frank exchange of innermost feelings. If the other person is resistant or continually evasive on this score, the limits of tolerance may eventually be breached. The outcome will eventually be an unhappy marriage which in turn may end in divorce.

It seems that unhappy marriages have long been with us, and may continue so to be. John Milton, in *The Doctrine and Discipline of Divorce*, has this to say:

> What thing more instituted to the solace and delight of man than marriage? and yet the misinterpreting of some Scripture directed mainly against the abusers of the Law for divorce given by Moses, hath changed the blessing of matrimony not seldom into a familiar and co-inhabiting mischief; at least into a drooping and disconsolate household captivity, without refuge or redemption . . . For although God in the first ordaining of marriage, taught us to what end he did it, in words expressly implying the apt and cheerful conversation of man with woman, to comfort and refresh him against the evil of solitary life, not mentioning the purpose of generation till afterwards, as being but a secondary end in dignity, though not in necessity; yet now, if any two be but once handed in the Church, and have tasted in any sort the nuptial bed, let them find themselves never so mistaken in their dispositions through any error, concealment, or misadventure,

that through their different tempers, thoughts, and constitutions, they can neither be to one another a remedy against loneliness, nor live in any union or contentment all their days; yet they shall, so they be but found suitably weapon'd to the least possibility of sensual enjoyment, be made, despite antipathy, to fadge together, and combine as they may to their unspeakable wearisomeness and despair of all sociable delight in the ordinance which God established to that very end.

Milton's glorious prose expresses a heartfelt paradox: that God himself ordained marriage for mutual 'solace and delight', and yet the experience of marriage can often be one of 'a drooping and disconsolate household captivity'. Arnold Bennett, as we have seen, expressed much the same observation four centuries later, but from an atheistical-scientific point of view. We propose, therefore, however paradoxically, to commence our selective journey around marriage with those who have resisted it as an institution.

James McNeill Whistler, the American painter who made his home in Chelsea in the mid-nineteenth century, and whose flamboyant lifestyle included his suing John Ruskin for defamatory criticism of his art (Whistler was awarded a farthing damages in the civil court, which coin he afterwards wore on his watch-chain), was resistant to marriage. E. R. and J. Pennell, in *The Life of James McNeill Whistler*, report:

'I don't marry,' Whistler said, 'though I tolerate those who do.' But before he left the British Artists he did marry . . . Mr Labouchere holds himself responsible . . .

'I believe that I am responsible for his marriage to the widow of Mr Godwin, the architect. She was a remarkably pretty woman and very agreeable, and both she and he were thorough Bohemians. I was dining with them and some others one evening at Earl's Court. They were obviously greatly attracted to each other, and in a vague sort of way they thought of marrying. So I took the matter in hand to bring things to a practical point. "Jemmy," I said, "will you marry Mrs Godwin?" "Certainly," he replied. "Mrs Godwin," I said, "will you marry Jemmy?" "Certainly," she replied. "When?" I asked. "Oh, some day," said Whistler. "That won't do," I said, "we must have a date." So they both agreed that I should choose the day, what church to come to for the ceremony, provide the clergyman, and give the bride away. I fixed an early date, and got the then Chaplain of the House of Commons [the Rev. Mr Byng] to perform the ceremony. It took place a few days later.

'After the ceremony was over, we adjourned to Whistler's studio, where he had prepared a banquet. The banquet was on the table, but there were no chairs. So we sat on packing-cases . . . How unpractical they were was shown when I happened to meet the bride the day before the marriage in the street:

' "Don't forget to-morrow," I said. "No," she replied, "I am just going to buy my trousseau." "A little late for that, is it not?" I asked. "No," she answered, "for I am only going to buy a new toothbrush and a new sponge, as one ought to have new ones when one marries."'

Whistler was devoted to his wife, who henceforth occupied a far more prominent position in his life than could have been imagined. Indeed, his life was entirely changed by his marriage. He went less into society and had less time for his art . . . Not that Mrs Whistler was indifferent to his art. She was sympathetic. He liked to have her in the studio; when she could not come he brought the pictures he was painting home for her to see. He consulted her in his difficulties, she shared his troubles, she rejoiced in his triumphs.

An American female writer wrote an anonymous account of her feelings about marriage for the *Nation* in 1927. She also was resistant to marriage; but the outcome was happy:

> My parents were unhappily married. From this reality I was not guarded. Popular books in the field of child study were not available at the time, and my mother, in unburdening her mind to me, probably had no conception of the effect her confidences had. In all the struggles between my father and my mother I identified myself completely with her, and always thought him in the wrong. One day I heard her tell him that only the thought of my welfare prevented her from seeking a divorce. I solemnly assured her that I, too, could do without him and from then on I continually urged her to follow this course. When I was a sophomore in high school my mother acted upon this advice and the figure of my father passed out of our lives.
>
> But the shadow of those early experiences darkened my attitude toward men and marriage long after. I was sure that I should never marry, never give any man an opportunity to ruin my life . . . But with the biology and psychology courses of college and university, sex took on a new meaning. It was . . . a shock to me to learn that women had their share of the sexual instincts and emotions . . . It took many hours and days of reading to furnish me with a background against which I could evolve a new philosophy . . .
>
> At last I emerged with a modified viewpoint. The necessity of a normal sex life for women was a scientific fact, and I must bow to the truths established by science. I was not, however, compelled to accept the institution of marriage, which was plainly a lineal descendant of primitive rites and ceremonials having its beginnings in ideas of magic later carried over into the folkways and mores. I could recognize that I had normal sex emotions

but I need not give up my freedom and independence by submitting to any such religious or legal ceremony. By this formula, I was able to preserve my guiding fiction intact.

It is amusing, now, to look back on this process of reassurance. Men and women are inevitably possessed of a power over each other which cannot be thought out of existence or evaded by refusing to legalize a relationship. Whether or not it is conventionalized, love has a coercive effect upon individual behaviour; refusal of marriage cannot alter this fact . . . Through a more scientific approach, I began to see things as they actually were rather than as I wished them to be. I even came to understand that in spite of the intensity of my feeling about marriage I might be able to accept the outward form so long as the inner spirit of the relationship embodied freedom. Thus, at thirty, I went forth to meet the fate which I had so long feared – and found it good!

It is fortunate for me that this venture has been with a man of insight, imagination, and humour, who cherishes no desire to be owner or tyrant. He respects my work as much as I do his. If he does not feel quite so keenly as I the need of economic independence after marriage, he is more eager that I have leisure for creative work than I am myself. Nor is this because my writings bear witness that I am his wife, for I keep my own name. To us, marriage is no sacred bond which it would be sacrilege to sever. Rather, we regard it as a form to which we have submitted because it is the only way in which we can give expression to our love without interference. With marriage, thus interpreted, I am content. It is as if I had accomplished the impossible feat of eating my cake and having it – for I have both love and freedom, which once seemed to me such incompatible bedfellows.

William Godwin (1756–1836) is described by Lord Birkenhead in his anthology, *The Five Hundred Best English Letters* (Cassell, 1931), as 'a man of strongly revolutionary principles, including a contempt for marriage, and he encouraged similar opinions in his friend and disciple Shelley. The fact gives added piquancy to the following letter to a woman friend (Mary Hays), announcing his marriage to Mary Wollstonecraft, the feminist authoress, who professed the same views':

> My fair neighbour desires me to announce to you a piece of news, which it is consonant to the regard that she and I entertain for you, you should learn rather from us than from any other quarter. She bids me remind you of the earnest way in which you pressed me to prevail upon her to change her name [to revert to her own name of Wollstonecraft instead of Imlay, her name upon first marriage]; she directs me to add that it has happened to me, like many other disputants, to be entrapped in my own toils; in short, that we found that there was no way so obvious for her to drop the name of Imlay, as to assume the name of Godwin. Mrs Godwin (who the devil is she?) will be glad to see you at No. 29 Polygon, Somers Town, whenever you are inclined to favour her with a call.

Elizabeth Barrett, poet, who was later to marry the poet Robert Browning and with him to find ecstatic happiness, wrote on 1 September 1831:

> I dreamt last night that I was married, just married; & in an agony to procure a dissolution of the engagement. Scarcely ever considered my single state with more satisfaction than when I awoke! – I never *will* marry: but if I ever were to do such a foolish thing, I hope I may not feel as I did last night!

Regina Barreca, the American author, in *Perfect Husbands (and Other Fairy Tales)* writes:

> Very likely, a man who is unsteady, immature, and selfish will not be transformed into a terrific husband just because he has signed off on the wedding contract. Many men feel as if they can hold on to their deepest wishes and greatest freedoms only if they remain single because entering into marriage assumes that they will become dutiful, responsible – and fettered.

> Miss Jackson is married to young Mr Gunthorpe, & is to be very unhappy. He swears, drinks, is cross, jealous, selfish & Brutal; the match makes *her* family miserable, & has occasioned *his* being disinherited.
>
> FROM A LETTER FROM JANE AUSTEN TO HER SISTER CASSANDRA, 8 FEBRUARY 1807

Not only Jane Austen would believe 'young Mr Gunthorpe' to be a poor candidate for marriage. Clearly he went beyond Miss Jackson's limits of tolerance. Behaviour within marriage, and behaviour towards one's spouse, is a fundamental aspect of the marriage contract and is implicit in the marriage vows: to love, honour and cherish.

> The sensible thing to do is to marry a man of exceptional character and unquestionable ugliness, so that a substantial affection may grow from prosaic reality. Such emotional ties can take many years to develop, which is why both men and women should delay marriage until their feelings are tried and tested . . .
>   Marriage is dangerous because it can be an escape from reality, a refuge from the important problems of life. But these things have to be faced eventually. I once had a woman friend who went from husband to husband because

she said it blotted out everything else. Love, then, is intellectual and emotional paralysis – pleasant enough in the short term, perhaps, but disastrous in the form of a prolonged legal dose.

PETRONELLA WYATT IN THE *INDEPENDENT*, 28 MARCH 1997

Courtship

The Passionate Shepherd to his Love

Come live with me and be my love,
And we will all the pleasures prove
That valleys, groves, hills, and fields,
Woods, or steepy mountain yields.

And we will sit upon the rocks,
Seeing the shepherds feed their flocks,
By shallow rivers to whose falls
Melodious birds sing madrigals.

And I will make thee beds of roses
And a thousand fragrant posies
A cap of flowers, and a kirtle
Embroidered all with leaves of myrtle;
. . .

A belt of straw and ivy buds,
With coral clasps and amber studs:
And if these pleasures may thee move,
Come live with me, and be my love.

CHRISTOPHER MARLOWE

The Nymph's Reply to the Shepherd

> If all the world and love were young,
> And truth in every shepherd's tongue,
> These pretty pleasures might me move
> To live with thee and be my love.
>
> . . .
>
> The flowers do fade, and wanton fields
> To wayward winter reckoning yields;
> A honey tongue, a heart of gall,
> Is fancy's spring, but sorrow's fall.
>
> . . .
>
> Thy belt of straw and ivy buds,
> Thy coral clasps and amber studs,
> All these in me no means can move
> To come to thee and be thy love.
>
> But could youth last and love still breed
> Had joys no date nor age no need,
> Then these delights my mind might move
> To live with thee and be thy love.

SIR WALTER RALEIGH

In this exchange between the passionate shepherd and the nymph, the shepherd is rejected, no doubt to woo afresh elsewhere: the nymph sees beyond his promised pleasures and presents. She cannot be sure of his heart; she knows that old age will come when the joys of love must give way to 'need'.

Set me in heaven, in earth, or else in hell,
In hill, or dale, or in the foaming flood;
Thrall, or at large, alive whereso I dwell,
Sick, or in health, in evil fame or good,
Hers will I be; and only with this thought
Content myself, although my chance be nought.

HENRY HOWARD, EARL OF SURREY

Were I as base as is the lowly plain
And you, my love, as high as heav'n above,
Yet should the thoughts of me your humble swain
Ascend to heav'n in honour of my love.
Were I as high as heav'n above the plain,
And you, my love, as humble and as low
As are the deepest bottoms of the main,
Wheresoe'er you were, with you my love should go.
Were you the earth, dear love, and I the skies,
My love should shine on you like to the sun,
And look upon you with ten thousand eyes,
Till heav'n waxed blind and till the world were dun.
Wheresoe'er I am, below or else above you,
Wheresoe'er you are, my heart shall truly love you.

JOSHUA SYLVESTER

The fountains mingle with the river
  And the rivers with the ocean,
The winds of heaven mix for ever
  With a sweet emotion;
Nothing in the world is single;
  All things by a law divine
In one another's being mingle
  Why not I with thine?

Marriage

See the mountains kiss high heaven
    And the wives clasp one another;
No sister-flower would be forgiven
    If it disdained its brother;
And the sunlight clasps the earth
    And the moonbeams kiss the sea:
What are all these kissings worth
    If thou kiss not me?

PERCY BYSSHE SHELLEY

Let us ... think only of the blessings that providence may yet have in store for us and that we may yet possess. I am happy in love – an affection exceeding a thousand times my deserts, which has continued so many years, and is yet undiminished ... Never will I marry in this world if I marry not you. Truly can I say that for the seven years since I avowed my love for you, I have ... forgone all company, and the society of all females (except my own relations) for your sake.

I am still ready to make my sacrifice for you ... I will submit to any thing you may command me – but cease to respect, to love and adore you I never can or will ... Believe me, my beloved & ever dearest Maria ...

JOHN CONSTABLE TO MARIA BICKNELL, 27 FEBRUARY 1816;
THEY MARRIED IN OCTOBER 1816

When Henry told me he cared for me, that unstifled inner voice which we all of us hear more or less distinctly told me I would be untrue to myself and quite unworthy of life if, when such a man came knocking at the door, I did not fling it wide open.

MARGOT ASQUITH

87

As he drew near her his grave discretion passed from him as clouds pass from a hillside. She smiled radiantly. He held out both his hands for both of hers and never did a maiden come so near and yet not get a public and shameless kissing.

One could as soon describe music as tell their conversation. It was a matter of tones and feelings. But the idea of flight together, of the bright awakening in unfamiliar sunshine with none to come between them had gripped them both.

H. G. WELLS, *MARRIAGE*

She wasn't to be married tamely after the common fashion which trails home and all one's beginnings into the new life. She was to be eloped with, romantically and splendidly, into a glorious new world. She walked on shining clouds, and if she felt some remorse, it was a very tender and satisfactory remorse, and with a clear conviction below it that in the end she would be forgiven.

H. G. WELLS, *MARRIAGE*

'Oh, 'tis time I should talk to your mother,
Sweet Mary,' says I.
'Oh, don't talk to my mother,' says Mary,
Beginning to cry:
'For my mother says men are deceivers,
And never, I know, will consent;
She says girls in a hurry who marry,
At leisure repent.'

'Then, suppose I would talk to your father,
Sweet Mary,' says I.
'Oh, don't talk to my father,' says Mary,
Beginning to cry:
'For my father he loves me so dearly,

He'll never consent I should go –
If you talk to my father,' says Mary.
'He'll surely say, "No".'

'Then how shall I get you, my jewel?
Sweet Mary,' says I;
'If your father and mother's so cruel,
Most surely I'll die.'
'Oh, never say die, dear,' says Mary;
'A way now to save you I see:
Since my parents are both so contrary –
You'd better ask me!'

SAMUEL LOVER

Since first I saw your face I resolved
To honour and renown you;
If now I be disdained, I wish
My heart had never known you.
What, I that loved and you that liked
Shall we begin to wrangle?
No, no, no, my heart is fast
And cannot disentangle.

The sun whose beams most glorious are
Rejecteth no beholder;
And thy sweet beauty, past compare,
Makes my poor eyes the bolder.
Where beauty moves and wit delights
And signs of kindness bind me,
There, oh there, where'er I go
I leave my heart behind me.

FORD

My dearest you know you have no idea how fond I am of
you – because when things are really serious with me I

become reserved about them. And I feel so dreadfully that you do not care nearly as much for me. There are such heaps of signs that you don't: your letting me go away so easily, and your being cross with me about getting my hair cut.

Darling, I know these things are absurd, and I don't mind really, as all I want is for you to let me adore you: and then, when we are married, perhaps you will get to care for me too. I mean really care – not just like. Except I know you care more than just like already, but it is not that absolute abandonment of self which I feel.

Darling, it was so nice when I was tired yesterday and you let me put my head on your shoulder.

HAROLD NICOLSON TO VITA SACKVILLE-WEST,
19 SEPTEMBER 1913

See also Vita Sackville-West's letters to him during their marriage, pages 174–6.

[Mr Darcy:] 'You are too generous to trifle with me. If your feelings are still what they were last April, tell me so at once. *My* affections and wishes are unchanged; but one word from you will silence me on this subject for ever.'

Elizabeth, feeling all the more than common awkwardness and anxiety of his situation, now forced herself to speak; and immediately, though not very fluently, gave him to understand that her sentiments had undergone so material a change since the period to which he alluded, as to make her receive with gratitude and pleasure his present assurances. The happiness which this reply produced was such as he had probably never felt before, and he expressed himself on the occasion as sensibly and as warmly as a man violently in love can be supposed to do. Had Elizabeth been able to encounter his eyes, she might have seen how well the expression of heartfelt delight diffused over his face became him; but, though she could not look, she could listen, and he told her of feelings which, in proving of what importance she was to him, made his affection every moment more valuable.

JANE AUSTEN, *PRIDE AND PREJUDICE*

At about half past twelve I sent for Albert; he came to the Closet where I was alone, and after a few minutes I said to him, that I thought he must be aware *why* I wished them to come here – and that it would make me *too happy* if he would consent to what I wished (to marry me). We embraced each other, and he was *so* kind, *so* affectionate. I told him I was quite unworthy of him – he said he would be very happy '*das Leben mit dir zu zubringen*' [to go through life with you], and was so kind, and seemed so happy, that I really felt it was the happiest brightest moment in my life. I told him it was a great sacrifice – which he wouldn't allow; I then told him of the necessity of keeping it a secret, except to his father and Uncle Leopold and Stockmar, to whom he said he would send a Courier next day – and also that it was to be as early as the beginning of February . . . I feel the happiest of human beings.

QUEEN VICTORIA, 15 OCTOBER 1839

Madam, It is the hardest thing in the world to be in love, and yet attend business. As for me, all who speak to me find out, and I must lock myself up, or other people will do it for me.

A gentleman asked me this morning, 'What news from Lisbon?' and I answered, 'She is exquisitely handsome.' Another desired to know 'when I had last been at Hampton Court?' I replied, 'It will be on Tuesday come se'nnight.'

Pr'ythee allow me at least to kiss your hand before that day, that my mind may be in some composure. O Love!

> A thousand torments dwell about thee,
> Yet who could live, to live without thee?

Methinks I could write a volume to you; but all the language on earth would fail in saying how much, and with what disinterested passion, I am ever yours.

SIR RICHARD STEELE, FOUNDER OF *TATLER AND THE SPECTATOR*
TO MRS SCURLOCK, WHO BECAME HIS SECOND WIFE,
1 SEPTEMBER 1707

What little attempt Henry Grantly then made . . . need not be explained with minuteness. But I think that his first effort was not successful. Grace was embarrassed and retreated, and it was not till she had been compelled to give a direct answer to a direct question that she submitted to allow his arm round her waist. But when she had answered that question she was almost more humble than becomes a maiden who has just been wooed and won. A maiden who has been wooed and won, generally thinks that it is she who has conquered, and chooses to be triumphant accordingly. But Grace was even mean enough to thank her lover. 'I do not know why you should be so good to me,' she said.

'Because I love you,' said he, 'better than all the world.'

'But why should you be so good to me as that? Why should you love me? I am such a poor thing for a man like you to love.'

'I have had the wit to see that you are not a poor thing, Grace; and it is thus that I have earned my treasure. Some girls are poor things, and some are rich treasures.'

'If love can make me a treasure, I will be your treasure.

> And if love can make me rich, I will be rich for you.'
> ANTHONY TROLLOPE, *THE LAST CHRONICLE OF BARSET*

Me darlin Love, me lickle Dove,
Me dumplin, me gizada,
Me Sweety Sue, I goes for you
Like how flies goes for sugar.

As ah puts me pen to paper
An me pen nib start to fly,
Me remembrance remember
De fus day you ketch me y'eye.

You did just come off o' tram-car,
A bus was to you right,
A car swips pass you lef-aise
An you stan up stiff wid fright!

You jaw drop, you mout open,
Jus like wen jackass start yawn,
Me heart go boogoo-boogoo
An ah know wha meck ah born!

Noh scorn me lickle letter Love,
Noh laugh after me yaw,
Me larnin not too good, but wat
Me kean spell, me wi draw!

De ting eena de corner wid
De freckles is me heart,
An de plate o' yam an salfish mean
Dat we can never part.

See how me draw de two face dem
Dah-look pon one anada
Well one is you an one is me,
Teck anyone you rada!

Is not a cockroach foot dis, is
A finger wid a ring,
An it mean ah want to married you
Dis line is piece o' string.

Teck it put roun de wedden-finger
A you wedden-han,
Careful fe get de right size, an
Den gi it to dis man.

De man is me. Now sweet-rice,
Keep swell til ah see you nex',
Accep me young heart wile ah close
Wid love an bans o' X

LOUISE BENNETT, JAMAICAN DIALECT

Love not me for comely grace
For my pleasing eye or face;
Nor for any outward part,
No, nor for my constant heart;
  For those may fail or turn to ill,
    So thou and I shall sever.
Keep therefore a true woman's eye,
And love me still, but know not why;
  So hast thou the same reason still
    To dote upon me ever.

ANON.

You only have revealed me to myself, for without your aid
my best knowledge of myself would have been merely to
know my own shadow – to watch it flickering on the wall,
and mistake its fantasies for my own real actions. Do you
comprehend what you have done for me?

NATHANIEL HAWTHORNE TO SOPHIA PEABODY

We seem to have been translated to the other state of being, without having passed through death . . . It is usually supposed that the cares of life come with matrimony but I seem to have cast off all cares.

NATHANIEL HAWTHORNE, in his diary after their marriage

If any young Miss reads this autobiography and wants a little advice from a very old hand, I will say to her, when a man threatens to commit suicide after you have refused him, you may be quite sure that he is a vain, petty fellow or a great goose; if you felt any doubts about your decision before, you need have none after this and under no circumstances must you give way. To marry a man out of pity is folly; and, if you think you are going to influence the kind of fellow who has 'never had a chance, poor devil,' you are profoundly mistaken. One can only influence the strong characters in life, not the weak; and it is the height of vanity to suppose that you can make an honest man of anyone.

MARGOT ASQUITH

If you choose a girl in this country [the writer is referring to the African country where he was working] as your wife, or would-be wife, you do not choose just this individual person, isolated from everything else. You choose her with her education, her tastes, her likes and dislikes, her habits and customs, in short, with her culture . . . I conclude that you might love her as an individual, her beauty and character, but you don't love her with her culture.

. . . real love means to love her with her background, her culture. A big wedding feast belongs to this culture. If you marry a girl from this country, then you must accept this fact. More than that – you must not only accept it un-grudgingly, you must even like it.

. . . marriage is a burden, a responsibility, even under normal circumstances. This additional burden of cultural differences is often the straw that breaks the camel's back. What makes these marriages break down is the fact that the partners do not fully accept each other's different cultures. This may start with tiny things, such as the likes and dislikes of certain foods or the way of preparing them – and it may end with a different outlook on life as a whole.

WALTER TROBISCH, *I MARRIED YOU*

The difficulties in the way of early marriage are real and hard to overcome. Every couple has to decide whether to wait for an added degree of financial security, or whether to marry without much security, often in difficult circumstances and often with the wife continuing to earn her living. It is a problem which can only be decided by each individual couple according to their own scale of values . . . The early struggles faced in a spirit of adventure can do much to unite husband and wife, and to lay a sure foundation on which to build up the family life of the future. For all young couples the task is fundamentally the same – to follow the light as they see it, and to be prepared to work and sacrifice for the attainment of an ideal.

SOCIETY OF FRIENDS, *MARRIAGE AND PARENTHOOD*, 1954

In looking forward to marriage, remember that happiness depends on the presence of a reverent and understanding love. Consider the serious responsibilities of parenthood, and do not forget the help you may draw from the loving counsel of your own parents. Seek to be joined in a common discipleship of Jesus Christ. Ask guidance of God, desiring, above all temporal considerations, that your union may be owned and blest of Him.

SOCIETY OF FRIENDS, *GENERAL ADVICES*, 1928

The union of husband and wife is fraught with momentous issues, and is not to be thought of lightly. Happiness and blessing in marriage depend first on the presence of devoted love, a love which is not the outcome of a merely passing attraction, but which includes a real respect by each for the personality of the other. Every such union should be undertaken in the fear of the Lord, and with a reverent attention to His counsel and guidance. It will be owned and blessed by Him if the healthy love that draws two human souls together is sanctified by the larger love of Christ and of His brethren; it will yield its fairest fruit as it is chastened by the discipline of care and trial bravely borne, and ripened into self-forgetting devotion by the mutual influence of parents and children. The family is the standing witness that man is not intended to live alone: that he becomes what he is meant to be as his character is trained in unselfishness by responsibility for others, and by the claims and duties of a common life.

SOCIETY OF FRIENDS, 1911, 1925

Henry and Catherine were married, the bells rang and everybody smiled; and as this took place within a twelve-month from the first day of their meeting, it will not appear, after all the dreadful delays occasioned by the General's cruelty, that they were essentially hurt by it. To begin perfect happiness at the respective ages of twenty-six and eighteen, is to do pretty well; and professing myself more-over, convinced that the General's unjust interference, so far from being really injurious to their felicity, was perhaps rather conducive of it, by improving their knowledge of each other, and adding strength to their attachment, I leave

97

it to be settled by whomsoever it may concern, whether the tendency of this work be altogether to recommend parental tyranny, or reward filial disobedience.

JANE AUSTEN, *NORTHANGER ABBEY*

Love

There is a difference between the two Greek words for love, *eros* and *agape*. Each has their champions, who claim that one or the other is the only real way of experiencing love, for indeed each has its very special beauty, truth and worth. Proponents of each would describe being in love as:

> *Eros*: Real love is an all-consuming, desperate yearning for the beloved, who is perceived as different, mysterious, and elusive. The depth of love is measured by the intensity of obsession with the loved one. There is little time or attention for other interests or pursuits, because so much energy is focused on recalling past encounters or imagining future ones. Often, great obstacles must be overcome, and thus there is an element of suffering in true love. Another indication of the depth of love is the willingness to endure pain and hardship for the sake of the relationship. Associated with real love are feelings of excitement, rapture, drama, anxiety, tension, mystery, and yearning.

> *Agape*: Real love is a partnership to which two caring people are deeply committed. These people share many basic values, interests, and goals, and tolerate good-naturedly their individual differences. The depth of love is measured by the mutual trust and respect they feel toward each other. Their relationship allows each to be more fully expressive, creative, and productive in the world. There is much joy in shared experiences both past and present, as

well as those that are anticipated. Each views the other as his/her dearest and most cherished friend. Another measure of the depth of love is the willingness to look honestly at oneself in order to promote the growth of the relationship and the deepening of intimacy. Associated with real love are feelings of serenity, security, devotion, understanding, companionship, mutual support, and comfort.

ROBIN NORWOOD, *WOMEN WHO LOVE TOO MUCH*

If an individual is able to love productively, he loves himself too; if he can love only others, he cannot love at all.

ERICH FROMM, *THE ART OF LOVING*

Love is moral even without legal marriage, but marriage is immoral without love.

ELLEN KEY, *THE MORALITY OF WOMAN*

I have no scruple in saying that you cannot be in Love. My dear Fanny, I am ready to laugh at the idea – and yet it is no laughing matter to have had you so mistaken as to your own feelings – And with all my heart I wish I had cautioned you on that point when first you spoke to me; but tho' I did not think you then so *much* in love as you thought yourself, I did consider you as being attached in a degree – quite sufficiently for happiness, as I had no doubt it would increase with opportunity. And from the time of our being in London together, I thought you really very much in love – But you certainly are not at all – there is no concealing it. What strange creatures we are! It seems as if your being secure of him (as you say yourself) had made you Indifferent. – There was a little disgust I suspect, at the Races – & I do not wonder at it. His expressions there would not do for one who had rather more Acuteness, Penetration & Taste, than Love, which was your case. And yet, after all, I *am* surprised that the change in your feelings should be so great. He is, just what he ever was, only more evidently & uniformly devoted to *you*. This is all the difference. How shall we account for it? . . . Poor dear Mr J. P.! Oh! dear Fanny, your mistake has been one that thousands of women fall into. He was the *first* young Man who attached himself to you. That was the charm, & most powerful it is . . .

JANE AUSTEN TO HER NIECE, FANNY KNIGHT,
18 NOVEMBER 1814

Courage and strength are not on the typical list of requirements for a marriage, but perhaps they should be. Perhaps courage, strength, an ability to learn from experience, and a sense of humor should be added to the prenuptial checklist. Examining the relationship of men and women within a larger context will inevitably inform the way we deal with one another on an intimate basis. Once we can see how our most individual actions are informed by forces of which we might not even have been aware, we can make our choices with more insight.

REGINA BARRECA, *PERFECT HUSBANDS (AND OTHER FAIRY
TALES)*

Faith describes her intentions:

I'd loved him for years and I wanted the world to know we weren't just a couple for the sake of convenience, although no doubt many marriages are just that. But I wanted to be able to shout from the rooftops that not only was this for good – it was for better and for worse. I wanted to make a new family out of the combination of our lives. I wanted our relatives to be related to one another. I wanted to be able to use all the usual terms: sister-in-law, niece, stepchild, whatever. Names and naming are important and should not be underestimated. The first time I heard his adult daughter describe me as her stepmother, we both laughed at the connotations but it was still a relief to have a name for what we were to each other. Suddenly we were also legitimate and official.

REGINA BARRECA, *PERFECT HUSBANDS (AND OTHER FAIRY TALES)*

Taking control of our own lives – even and especially when we are married – has nothing to do with a lack or a distrust of love. Quite the opposite, in loving ourselves enough to care for the independent person we were always meant to be, we are better able to love others.

REGINA BARRECA, *PERFECT HUSBANDS (AND OTHER FAIRY TALES)*

There is nothing like the sight of a lovely Woman! Nothing so subdues one, so controls one; I feel the influence of her eyes if they wander down my form just like electrical air from a point. I sat by one this morning at a lecture . . . and without one atom of appetite or passion felt an affectionate desire to put her sweet arm round my neck and nestle my own cheek on her lovely bosom – with pure heartfelt softness. She looked so gentle, so delicate, so soft, so yielding, that one's manly feelings of protection were roused, and one's gentle emotions of tenderness were excited.

The principle implanted by Nature that the feelings of consciousness as to manhood should be increased by gratifying the other Sex, often pushes us to the gratification without reference to the object for which that sensation was given.

B. R. HAYDON, 8 APRIL 1815

How happy the lover,
   How easy his chain,
   How pleasing his pain!
How sweet to discover
   He sighs not in vain.
For love ev'ry creature
Is form'd by his nature;
No joys are above
The pleasures of love.

In vain are our graces,
   In vain are your eyes,
   If love you despise;
When age furrows faces,
   'Tis time to be wise.
Then use the short blessing,
That flies in possessing:
No joys are above
The pleasures of love.

JOHN DRYDEN

At length their long kiss severed, with sweet smart:
   And as the last slow sudden drops are shed
   From sparkling eaves when all the storm has fled,
So singly flagged the pulses of each heart.
Their bosoms sundered, with the opening start
   Of married flowers to either side outspread
   From the knit stem; yet still their mouths, burnt red,
Fawned on each other where they lay apart.

Sleep sank them lower than the tide of dreams,
   And their dreams watched them sink, and slid away.
Slowly their souls swam up again, through gleams
   Of watered light and dull drowned waifs of day;

Till from some wonder of new woods and streams
  He woke, and wondered more: for there she lay.
                                        DANTE GABRIEL ROSSETTI

It is in the hour of fulfilment of love between a man and a woman that the reckless affirmations of mutinous life may best be apprehended. It is then that the vain mind of man, confounded utterly by the roarings of desire, lies open at last to instruction from the senses, from those five un-paragoned wits that have become in one snatched instant more piercingly sensible of God's true word than ever are the pelts of frogs to a touch from mortal fingers hot as fire. With lips pressed upon lips and with bodies of tragic flesh fast clinging, the Platonic ordinance is suddenly revoked, and spontaneously our separated halves spring back once more to their right predestined wholes. And what is con-tained in these supreme transports, as hollow of thought as they are deep charged with feeling? A single spirit of splendour, we hunt in triumph through forests of flame. We are the wind that bends the flower at the hour before day-break, the wave that shakes the firm rock, the forked lightning that cleaves the tree, down, down to the matrix of its roots. It is you that I am possessing. It is you to whom I give myself utterly, utterly. As two we met, but as one we are parted.

                                        LLEWELYN POWYS, *LOVE AND DEATH*

The gratification of the senses soon becomes a very small part of that profound and complicated sentiment which we call Love. Love, on the contrary, is a universal thirst for a communion, not merely of the senses, but of our whole nature, intellectual, imaginative and sensitive. He who finds his antitype [the person who complements him perfectly], enjoys a love perfect and enduring; time cannot change it, distance cannot remove it; the sympathy is complete.

BENJAMIN DISRAELI, *HENRIETTA TEMPLE*

From the moment I had seen her . . . I could think of nothing else. My whole approach to life was altered. I no longer cared whether I was to be a poet or not a poet, I no longer was concerned with the deeper problems of existence. Unless I could associate what I saw, heard, tasted, smelt, and touched with her I no longer gave it attention. What reason was there for me to heed the waves that broke day and night against the irregular coasts of the world, to exult in the grass that grew day and night upon the broad back of the stationary land, to watch from ancient elbow-bone bridges the flowing away of rivers, to look up at the crafty midnight stars, unless such appearances could be made to serve in some way as poetical settings for this girl of my utter idolatry? It seemed to me then, as indeed it seems to me still, that every inch of her body shone with some mysterious light . . . that she breathed, that she walked, that she slept to wake again, was an unending source of wonder to me.

LLEWELYN POWYS, *LOVE AND DEATH*

She was a phantom of delight
When first she gleamed upon my sight;
A lovely apparition, sent
To be a moment's ornament:
Her eyes as stars of twilight fair;
Like twilight's too her dusky hair;
But all things else about her drawn
From May-time and the cheerful dawn;
A dancing shape, an image gay,
To haunt, to startle, and way-lay.

WILLIAM WORDSWORTH

Marriage

I wonder, by my troth, what thou and I
Did, till we loved? were we not wean'd till then?
But suck'd on country pleasures, childishly?
Or snorted we in the Seven Sleepers' den?
'Twas so; but this, all pleasures fancies be;
If ever any beauty I did see,
Which I desired, and got, 'twas but a dream of thee.

JOHN DONNE

Never love unless you can
Bear with all the faults of man:
Men sometimes will jealous be,
Though but little cause they see;
   And hang the head, as discontent,
   And speak what straight they will repent.

Men that but one Saint adore,
Make a show of love to more:
Beauty must be scorn'd in none,
Though but truly serv'd in one:
   For what is courtship, but disguise?
   True hearts may have dissembling eyes.

Men when their affairs require,
Must a while themselves retire:
Sometimes hunt, and sometimes hawk,
And not ever sit and talk.
   If these, and such like you can bear,
   Then like, and love, and never fear.

THOMAS CAMPION

Now cease, my wandering eyes,
   Strange beauties to admire.
In change least comfort lies;
   Long joys yield long desires.
    One faith, one love
Makes our frail pleasures eternal, and in sweetness prove
    New hopes, new joys
Are still with sorrow declining unto deep annoys.

One man hath but one soul
   Which art cannot divide.
If all one soul must love
   Two loves must be denied.
    One soul, one love,
By faith and merit united cannot move.
    Distracted sprites
Are ever changing and hapless in their delights.

Nature two eyes hath given
   All beauty to impart
As well in earth as heaven;
   But she hath given one heart;
    That, though we see
Ten thousand beauties, yet in us one should be,
    One steadfast love,
Because our hearts stand fixed although our eyes do move.
JOHN DOWLAND, SECOND BOOK OF SONGS

Marriage

Sweet Woman's tongue! I love to hear its chime
That drowns the heavier iron tongue of time!
Rich in its tones, and varied in its power,
Its accents falling like an April shower
Upon the snow-drops of man's heart, to cheer,
Warm, soften, cherish, animate, endear!

JAMES BIRD

My Lord,

I wonder not at my love, but at yours, because the object
of mine is good. I wish the object of yours were so, yet
methinks, you should love nothing that were ill, therefore
if I have any part of good 'tis your love makes me so, but
loved I nothing else but you, I love all that is good, and
loving nothing above you I have love's recompense. My
lord, I have not had much experience of the world, yet I
have found it such as I could willingly part with it, but
since I knew you, I fear I shall love it too well, because you
are in it, and yet, methinks, you are not in it, because you
are not of it, a strong enchantment, but pray love so as you
may have me long, for I shall ever be, my lord, your most
humble servant

MARGARET LUCAS, WHO MARRIED WILLIAM CAVENDISH, LATER
DUKE OF NEWCASTLE, IN 1645

Esteem and regard may be without passion, but tenderness
and confidence, and what we call friendship among ourselves, will, with opportunity, turn to desire in the different
sexes. We desire to possess a friend to know their heart, to
be in their thoughts, this must turn to passion between the
sexes, I think 'tis impossible to be otherwise . . .

ANNE DONNELLAN TO ELIZABETH ROBINSON
(LATER MONTAGU), IN 1742

Weddings

Ah, love, let us be true
To one another! for the world, which seems
To lie before us like a land of dreams,
So various, so beautiful, so new,
Hath really neither joy, nor love, nor light,
Nor certitude, nor peace, nor help for pain:
And we are here as on a darkling plain
Swept with confused alarms of struggle and flight,
Where ignorant armies clash by night.

MATTHEW ARNOLD

It was a very cold evening and I felt very tired, but we went
down Weston Lane and looked at the stars. I said that the
happiness one got out of love was worth any unhappiness it
might (and generally does) bring. I can't remember what
Rupert said but he wasn't so sure about it . . .

BARBARA PYM, 21 SEPTEMBER 1932

If thou must love me, let it be for nought
Except for love's sake only. Do not say
'I love her for her smile . . . her look . . . her way
Of speaking gently . . . for a trick of thought
That falls in well with mine, and certes brought
A sense of pleasant ease on such a day' –
For these things in themselves, Beloved, may
Be changed, or change for thee, – and love, so wrought,
May be unwrought so. Neither love me for
Thine own dear pity's wiping my cheeks dry, –
A creature might forget to weep, who bore
Thy comfort long, and lose thy love thereby!
But love me for love's sake, that evermore
Thou mayst love on, through love's eternity.

ELIZABETH BARRETT BROWNING

Who is Silvia? what is she,
   That all our swains commend her?
Holy, fair and wise is she;
   The heaven such grace did lend her,
That she might admirèd be.

Is she kind as she is fair?
   For beauty lives with kindness:
Love doth to her eyes repair,
   To help him of his blindness;
And, being helped, inhabits there.

Then to Silvia let us sing,
   That Silvia is excelling;
She excels each mortal thing
   Upon the dull earth dwelling;
To her let us garlands bring.

WILLIAM SHAKESPEARE

'Fair, kind, and true,' is all my argument,
'Fair, kind, and true,' varying to other words;
And in this change is my invention spent,
Three themes in one, which wondrous scope affords.
   'Fair, kind, and true,' have often lived alone.
   Which three till now never kept seat in one.

WILLIAM SHAKESPEARE

Who is it that says most? which can say more
Than this rich praise, that you alone are you?

WILLIAM SHAKESPEARE

Shall I compare thee to a summer's day?
Thou art more lovely and more temperate:
Rough winds do shake the darling buds of May,
And summer's lease hath all too short a date:

Sometimes too hot the eyes of heaven shines,
And often is his gold complexion dimm'd,
And every fair from fair sometime declines,
By chance, or nature's changing course, untrimm'd;
But thy eternal summer shall not fade,
Nor lose possession of that fair thou ow'st;
Nor shall Death brag thou wander'st in his shade,
When in eternal lines to time thou grow'st:
　So long as men can breathe, or eyes can see,
　So long lives this, and this gives life to thee.

WILLIAM SHAKESPEARE

Let me not to the marriage of true minds
Admit impediments; love is not love
Which alters when it alteration finds,
Or bends with the remover to remove:
O, no! it is an ever-fixèd mark,
That looks on tempests and is never shaken;
It is the star to every wandering bark,
Whose worth's unknown, although his height be taken.
Love's not Time's fool, though rosy lips and cheeks
Within his bending sickle's compass come;
Love alters not with his brief hours and weeks,
But bears it out even to the edge of doom.
　If this be error and upon me prov'd,
　I never writ, nor no man ever lov'd.

WILLIAM SHAKESPEARE

She walks in beauty, like the night
　Of cloudless climes and starry skies;
And all that's best of dark and bright
　Meet in her aspect and her eyes:
Thus mellowed to that tender light
　Which heaven to gaudy day denies.

One shade the more, one ray the less,
    Had half impaired the nameless grace
Which waves in every raven tress,
    Or softly lightens o'er her face;
Where thoughts serenely sweet express
    How pure, how dear their dwelling-place.

LORD BYRON

My Love in her attire doth show her wit,
    It doth so well become her:
For every season she has dressings fit,
    For winter, spring and summer.
No beauty she doth miss,
    When all her robes are on:
But beauty's self she is,
    When all her robes are gone.

ANON.

But Love is a durable fire
    In the mind ever burning:
never sick never old never dead
    from itself never turning.

SIR WALTER RALEIGH

Never shall a young man
Thrown into despair
By those great honey-coloured
Ramparts at your ear,
Love you for yourself alone
And not your yellow hair.

But I can get a hair-dye
And set such colour there,
Brown, or black, or carrot,
That young men in despair
May love me for myself alone
And not my yellow hair.

I heard an old religious man
But yesternight declare
That he had found a text to prove
That only God, my dear,
Could love you for yourself alone
And not your yellow hair.

W. B. YEATS

At seventeen, he falls in love quite madly
  With eyes of tender blue.
At twenty-four, he gets it rather badly
  With eyes of a different hue.
At thirty-five, you'll find him flirting sadly
  With two, or three, or more.
When he fancies he is past love,
It is then he finds his last love,
And he loves her as he's never loved before.

OLD SONG

And *I* (if I am to be thought of) would be prouder to eat
cresses and macaroni (Dearest – there is a manufactory of
macaroni and writing-paper at Amalfi close by – observe
that combination! macaroni and writing-paper!) *I* would
be prouder to eat cresses and macaroni with *you* as *you*,
than to sit with diamonds in my ears, under the shelter of
the woolsack, *you* being a law-lord and parliamentary
making of speeches! By the way, I *couldn't* have diamonds

in my ears: they never were *bored* for it . . . as I never was *born* for it. A physical inaptitude, here too!

Ah – your head is 'dizzy' my beloved! Tell me how it is now. And tell me how your mother is. I think of you – love you. I, who am discontented with myself . . . self-condemned as unworthy of you, in all else . . . am yet satisfied with the *love* I have for you – it seems worthy of you, as far as an abstract affection can go, without taking notice of the personality loving.

Do you see the meaning through the mist? Do you accept

Your very own

BA

ELIZABETH BARRETT TO ROBERT BROWNING, 1 JULY 1846

Love is to feel you in my very heart and hold you there for ever, through all chance and earthly changes.

ROBERT BROWNING

But love me for love's sake, that evermore
Thou mayst love on, through love's eternity.

ELIZABETH BARRETT

Your love is his blue sky behind the trees:
And every moment, as it passes slow,
Is like some splendid tower that he sees
Against a dawning sun's eternal glow.

VICTOR GOLLANCZ

To argue from her [Johnson's wife] being much older than Johnson, or any other circumstances, that he could not really love her, is absurd; for love is not a subject of reasoning, but of feeling, and therefore there are no

113

common principles upon which one can persuade another concerning it. Every man feels for himself, and knows how he is affected by particular qualities in the person he admires, the impressions of which are too minute and delicate to be substantiated in language.

JAMES BOSWELL, *THE LIFE OF SAMUEL JOHNSON*

O pure of heart! thou need'st not ask of me
What this strong music in the soul may be!
What, and wherein it doth exist,
This light, this glory, this fair luminous mist,
This beautiful and beauty-making power.

Joy, virtuous Lady! Joy that ne'er was given
Save to the pure, and in their purest hour,
Life, and Life's effluence, cloud at once and shower,
Joy, Lady! is the spirit and the power,
Which wedding Nature to us gives in dower,
A new Earth and new Heaven,
Undreamt of by the sensual and the proud –
Joy is the sweet voice, Joy the luminous cloud –
We in ourselves rejoice!
And thence flows all that charms or ear or sight,
All melodies the echoes of that voice,
All colours a suffusion from that light.

SAMUEL TAYLOR COLERIDGE

One must learn to love, and go through a good deal of suffering to get to it, like any knight of the grail, and the journey is always *towards* the other soul, not away from it. Do you think love is an accomplished thing, the day it is recognized? It isn't. To love, you have to learn to understand the other, more than she understands herself, and to submit to her understanding of you. It is damnably difficult and painful, but it is the only thing which

endures. You mustn't think that your desire or your fundamental need is to make a good career, or to fill your life
with activity, or even to provide for your family materially. It isn't. Your most vital necessity in this life is that
you shall love your wife completely and implicitly and in
entire nakedness of body and spirit. Then you will have
peace and inner security, no matter how many things go
wrong.

D. H. LAWRENCE TO T. D. D., 7 JULY 1914

Love is life's end (an end, but never ending)
All joys, all sweets, all happiness awarding;
    Love is life's wealth
      (ne'er spent, but ever spending),
  More rich by giving, taking by discarding;
Love's life's reward, rewarded in rewarding;
    Then from thy wretched heart
      fond care remove;
    Ah, should thou live but once
      love's sweets to prove.
    Thou wilt not love to live unless
      thou live to love.

ANON.

Life, I repeat, is energy of love
Divine or human; exercised in pain,
In strife, and tribulation; and ordained,
If so approved and sanctified, to pass,
Through shades and silent rest, to endless joy.

WILLIAM WORDSWORTH

All thoughts, all passions, all delights,
Whatever stirs this mortal frame,
All are but ministers of Love,
   And feed his sacred flame.

SAMUEL TAYLOR COLERIDGE

For [love] is a fire that, kindling its first embers in the narrow nook of a private bosom, caught from a wandering spark out of another private heart, glows and enlarges until it warms and beams upon multitudes of men and women, upon the universal heart of all, and so lights up the whole world and all nature with its generous flames.

RALPH WALDO EMERSON

Love is the magician, the enchanter, that changes worthless things to joy, and makes right-royal kings and queens of common clay. It is the perfume of that wondrous flower, the heart, and without that sacred passion, that divine swoon, we are less than beasts: but with it, earth is heaven and we are gods.

R. G. INGERSOLL

They are in love, they have always been in love, although sometimes they would have denied it. And because they have been in love they have survived everything that life could throw at them . . .

ERNEST HAVEMANN

Love is a temporary madness, it erupts like volcanoes and then subsides. And when it subsides you have to make a decision. You have to work out whether your roots have so entwined together that it is inconceivable that you should ever part. Because this is what love is. Love is not breathlessness, it is not excitement, it is not the promulgation of

116

promises of eternal passion, it is not the desire to mate every second minute of the day, it is not lying awake at night imagining that he is kissing every cranny of your body. No, don't blush, I am telling you some truths. That is just being 'in love', which any fool can do. Love itself is what is left over when being in love has burned away, and this is both an art and a fortunate accident. Your mother and I had it, we had roots that grew towards each other underground, and when all the pretty blossom had fallen from our branches we found that we were one tree and not two. But sometimes the petals fall away and the roots have not entwined. Imagine giving up your home and your people, only to discover after six months, a year, three years, that the trees have had no roots and have fallen over. Imagine the desolation. Imagine the imprisonment.

LOUIS DE BERNIÈRES

It is not easy to describe goodness; it usually comes out smug, unadventurous and without humour or warmth. I have always wanted to write a story or a play about goodness, because, when I meet it, it has always attracted me more than anything else. But it is hard to put on paper. The goodness I mean is a sense of unchanging security, in the widest sense of wholeness; and it is never suspected by those who have it. It is their natural essence; their being expresses it, not in words but in attitudes and behaviour. I have met a lot of it, in a variety of people, but nowhere more consistently than in Reggie. But I don't know how to write about it without outlining, and the point about goodness is that it cannot be confined or described, it can only be sensed and experienced in relationship. It is one of the highest expressions of love – not as A loves B, but as love makes the world go round in a far wider context. I find it interesting that Reggie, who has no formal religious beliefs, never goes to church on his own, doesn't, as far as I know, pray much, yet is at the place most of the rest of us have to strive to reach. His behaviour is instinctively Christian. He is unaware of this and will be surprised to read it. I think he would say he does not believe in an ecclesiastical God but he does believe in Good.

JOYCE GRENFELL

On the main question I am absolutely clear: it is unfair to go away with a man, to let him make love to you unless you are *deeply willing* to be his lover completely. It is also, though more subtly, unfair to him to be his lover out of a kind of pity or condescension. He may not think this; but if he doesn't, something is lacking in him . . .

But . . . what I want to hear from you – rest from my weariness; the beating of my heart tells me that you are capable of the tenderness of love, and that you have this wonderful and precious thing to give me – and that you will. I want you to take me in your arms, to let me sleep in peace with you, to reassure me of the eternity of human love. I want, I need terribly, to believe in love between a man and woman again. Now that I know you have suffered the anguish of love, I am not afraid to speak.

JOHN MIDDLETON MURRY TO M. M. M.

All my life I had had my heroes, and in one sense John was, and always will be – for death makes no difference to love – my hero. All the pure flame of hero-worship I poured at his feet and always, yes, all our life together, it was the greatest privilege to be with him. Always I was aware of a sense of wonder that *he* could love *me*. And the certain knowledge that he did made that wonder an abiding joy . . . Falling in love with John turned me, in the twinkling of an eye, into a different kind of woman.

MARY MIDDLETON MURRY

The one thing of permanent value and significance I have achieved: the one thing worth listening to that I have to say: is that man-woman love is the supreme felicity, and thus it is attainable.

JOHN MIDDLETON MURRY

Our love is absolutely simple, yet it is surpassing. I can say with literal truth that every single moment of every single day is transformed with it. I live, we live, in a quite new dimension of experience in which the ordinary is magical. And so we have lived now for over six years, during which time the love has grown more all pervasive from month to month, from week to week. That is the simple fact; on any showing it is marvellous. Were I to die tonight the miracle has been. Nay, more, this miracle has happened through the greater part of a terrible war, for it was at the end of July 1939 that I knew I loved Mary, and that a clue had been placed in my hands which, if I followed it faithfully, would lead me, not perhaps to happiness, but to integrity and fulfilment. Here was offered to me that which I have sought all my life, and despaired of finding, come indeed to believe that it could not, did not exist. If I refused to seize and follow the golden thread – but it never entered my head to refuse it.

JOHN MIDDLETON MURRY

Now sleeps the crimson petal, now the white;
Nor waves the cypress in the palace walk;
Nor winks the gold fin in the porphyry font:
The fire-fly wakens: waken thou with me.

119

Now droops the milk white peacock like a ghost,
And like a ghost she glimmers on to me.

Now lies the Earth all Danae to the stars,
And all thy heart lies open unto me.

Now slides the silent meteor on, and leaves
A shining furrow, as thy thoughts in me.

Now folds the lily all her sweetness up,
And slips into the bosom of the lake:
So fold thyself, my dearest, thou, and slip
Into my bosom and be lost in me.

ALFRED, LORD TENNYSON

Thou art not gone being gone, where'er thou art.
Thou leav'st in him thy watchful eye, in him thy loving
heart.

RALPH WALDO EMERSON

Never marry but for love; but see that thou lovest what is
lovely.
He that minds a body and not a soul has not the better part
of that relation, and will consequently want the noblest
comfort of a married life.

Between a man and his wife nothing ought to rule but
love . . .
As love ought to bring them together, so it is the best way
to keep them well together,

A husband and wife that love and value one another show
their children that they should do so too.
Others visibly lose their authority in their families by their
contempt of one another; and teach their children to be
unnatural by their own examples.

Let not enjoyment lessen, but augment, affection; it being the basest of passions to like when we have not, what we slight when we possess.

Here it is we ought to search out our pleasure, where the field is large and full of variety, and of an enduring nature: sickness, poverty, or disgrace being not able to shake it, because it is not under the moving influences of worldly contingencies.

Nothing can be more entire and without reserve; nothing more zealous, affectionate and sincere; nothing more contented and constant than such a couple, nor no greater temporal felicity than to be one of them.

WILLIAM PENN

There is this only to be recorded, that never was there a passion more ardent and less idolatrous; he loved her better than his life, with inexpressible tenderness and kindness, had a most high obliging esteem of her, yet still considered honour, religion, and duty above her nor ever suffered the intrusion of such a dotage as should blind him from marking her imperfections . . .

LUCY HUTCHINSON

For ourselves, Frieda and I have struggled through some bad times into a wonderful naked intimacy, all kindled with warmth, that I know at last is love. I think I ought not to blame women, as I have done, but myself, for taking my love to the wrong woman, before now. Let every man find, keep on trying till he finds, the woman who can take him and whose love he can take, then who will grumble about men or about women. But the thing must be two-sided. At any rate, and whatever happens, I do love, and I am loved. I have given and I have taken – and that is eternal. Oh, if only people could marry properly; I believe in marriage.

D. H. LAWRENCE TO MRS S. A. HOPKIN 19 AUGUST 1912

The best way of forgiving is often enough to forget, or at all events to behave as if we had forgotten; and perhaps the largest and sweetest solution of all is to act in the spirit of the old French proverb, which says 'To love is to pardon everything.'

A. C. BENSON

Although I conquer all the earth
Yet for me there is only one city.
In that city there is for me only one house;
And in that house, one room only;
And in that room, a bed.
And one woman sleeps there,
The shining joy and jewel of all my kingdom.

ANON.

Wedding Services

And the Poor Dears haven't the shadow of a doubt they will live happily ever afterwards.

FROM A PRIVATE LETTER, USED ON FLYLEAF OF H. G. WELLS
MARRIAGE

John Betjeman and his daughter Candida attended her best friend Sally Weaver's wedding one June day at Uffington Parish Church. The poet celebrated the wedding in verse:

In summer wind the elm leaves sing,
    And sharp's the shade they're shedding,
And loud and soft the church bells ring
    For Sally Weaver's wedding.

With chasing light the meadows fill,
   The greenness growing greener,
As racing over White Horse Hill
   Come bluer skies and cleaner.

The chalk-white walls, the steaming thatch
   In rain-washed air are clearing,
And waves of sunshine run to catch
   The bride for her appearing.

Inside the church in every pew
   Sit old friends, older grown now;
Their children whom our children knew
   Have children of their own now.

The babies wail, the organ plays,
   Now thunderous, now lighter;
The brighter day of Sally's days
   Grows every moment brighter.

And all the souls of Uffington,
   The dead among the living,
Seem witnessing the rite begun
   Of taking and of giving.

The flying clouds! The flying years!
   This church of centuries seven!
Now new its weathered stone appears
   When vows are made in Heaven.

The poet Walter de la Mare, in the introduction to his anthology *Love*, writes of the traditional English wedding:

> The bridge between 'single' and 'married' spans life's most crucial Rubicon. It is one singularly easy to cross, but not to retraverse. No other venture in life promises so much, may achieve even more, or prove so disastrous. None the

less, the customary English wedding is apt to conceal its gravity. Like our merry Christmas, it is a medley of the Christian and the pagan, and may fail to suggest anything in the nature of a Mystery.

... It is a joyous occasion. A few tears have been shed at the forgotten solemnity and significance of the Service, thoughts have been thought, memories have come flocking into mind, sweet or bitter, tinged with melancholy, gratitude or regret; the human contents of the two aisles have been critically compared; the Address has been welcomed inversely to its duration; the bride has borne the bell away; the martial strains from the 'Dream' peal up out of the organ. And now the tables are groaning under their burden of presents, champagne and wedding cake; the bridegroom's Hat has been found; the symbolic confetti have been distributed; the car is at the door. The most decisive event in the lives of the two 'young people', of 'the happy pair', is over. Honeymoons are delicious. The Captains and the Kings, or their equivalents, depart. We have washed our hands, and follow them.

The more fashionable, expensive and expansive the modern wedding, the less somehow it may seem to have had either Eros or Romance for its guiding star... Still, if many waters cannot quench love, neither should a multitude of wedding-guests.

WALTER DE LA MARE

The bride being attired in a gown of sheep's russet, and a kirtle of fine worsted, attired with a 'billement' of gold, and her hair as yellow as gold, hanging down behind her, which was curiously combed and plaited, she was led to church between two sweet boys, with bride laces and rosemary tied about their silken sleeves. There was a fair bride-cup of silver gilt carried before her, wherein was a goodly branch of rosemary, gilded very fair, hung about with silken ribands of all colours. Musicians came next, then a group of maidens, some bearing great bride-cakes, others garlands of wheat finely gilded; and thus they passed into the church.

HISTORY OF JACK OF READING

The next day we all drove to York Minster for the royal wedding.

Everything perfectly organized and the ceremony, for me, very moving. Prince Eddie looked so exactly like his father. The Duchess's looks, poise and glorious dignity were infinitely touching. Prince Eddie had given me a wonderful seat in the choir where I could see everything perfectly. The reception was beautifully done. The Queen and Prince Philip were charming to me, although at one point I nearly knocked Her Gracious Majesty for a burton and some moth-balls bounced from my trouser pocket.

NOEL COWARD, ON THE OCCASION OF THE MARRIAGE OF EDWARD, DUKE OF KENT, TO KATHARINE WORSLEY, June 1961

Sir John Suckling's *Upon a Wedding* in seventeenth-century London does not give the parson much of a look-in:

At Charing Cross, hard by the way,
Where we, thou know'st, do sell our hay,
   There is a house with stairs;
And there did I see coming down
Such folk as are not in our town,
   Forty at least, in pairs.

Amongst the rest, one pest'lent fine
(His beard no bigger though than thine)
    Walked on before the rest:
Our landlord looks like nothing to him:
The King (God bless him) 'twould undo him,
    Should he go still so drest.

But wot you what? the youth was going
To make an end of all his wooing;
    The parson for him stay'd:
Yet by his leave, for all his haste,
He did not so much wish all past,
    Perchance, as did the maid.

Her cheeks so rare a white was on,
No daisy makes comparison,
    Who sees them is undone;
For streaks of red were mingled there
Such as are on a Catherine pear,
    The side that's next the sun.

Her mouth so small, when she does speak,
Thou'dst swear her teeth her words did break,
    That they might passage get;
But she so handled still the matter,
They came as good as ours, or better,
    And are not spent a whit.

Just in the nick the cook knocked thrice,
And all the waiters in a trice
    His summons did obey;
Each serving-man, with dish in hand,
Marched boldly up, like our trained band,
    Presented, and away.

When all the meat was on the table,
What man of knife or teeth was able
  To stay to be intreated?
And this the very reason was,
Before the parson could say grace,
  The company was seated.

Now hats fly off, and youths carouse;
Healths first go round, and then the house,
  The bride's came thick and thick;
And when 'twas name'd another's health,
Perhaps he made it hers by stealth;
  And who could help it, Dick?

On the sudden up they rise and dance;
Then sit again and sigh, and glance:
  Then dance again and kiss:
Thus several ways the time did pass,
Whilst ev'ry woman wished her place,
  And every man wished his.

By this time all were stol'n aside
To counsel and undress the bride;
  But that he must not know:
But yet 'twas thought he guess'd her mind,
And did not mean to stay behind
  Above an hour or so.

At length the candle's out, and now
All that they had not done they do.
  What that is, who can tell?
But I believe it was no more
Than thou and I have done before
  With Bridget and with Nell.

This was a memorable day – the most interesting, in my whole Life – It made me feel very strange – I was afraid to reflect or to think lest I should lose the courage which every Woman stands in need of on such an occasion – I was obliged to dress in a hurry to attend my little Catholic Priest who received my Confession, when that was over I found Robert and Walter already arrived – My dear Bridegroom was even perhaps more agitated than his Bride – We were instantly married by the Catholic Priest and no Woman ever pronounced her vows with a happier heart – Robert pronounced his with a firmness and at the same time a feeling which greatly affected me – We had but just time to breakfast, and then I had to dress for the second marriage – my *bridal array* consisted of a white satin under dress and a patent net over it, with a long veil – ... my heart beat when we entered the church, nor could I go thro' the second ceremony without feeling even more affected – Miss Poole had been married a few hours before me, and I signed my name under hers with a steadier hand – I can never forget Jack's kindness to me before we left the vestry – We immediately went to Argyle House where we had a cold collation – Nothing can exceed the kindness I met with from every member of Robert's family – presents were pouring upon me, and Mr de Beaujolois gave me a very handsome amethyst and diamond cross – at about four *the happy pair* set out for Lady Elizabeth Cole's house at Twickenham – My Sisters seemed to feel a great deal when I left them – But they knew I was happy.

EUGENIA CAMPBELL

Elisabeth and Hermann were married in the monastery church at Paleocastritsa [Corfu]. Some years earlier, her father had built, for himself and her, a house clinging to the hill above a small bay, some way north of the monastery

headland. The place could be reached only on foot, either
along a stretch of sea-shore and up a woodland path, or,
after a boat trip round to the bay, almost perpendicularly
up from the sea . . .

The house looks out on a scene of powerful beauty, which
at night and in time of storm can turn to menace . . . The
restless Ionian nags incessantly at the coves and points.
Almost always there is the noise of the swell running in
from Italy and breaking over the rocks. Yet beside the house
a small vineyard has been planted, and scrub and cliff
flowers have found footholds all the way down to the
bay . . .

From this eyrie, Elisabeth's father had had the fancy to
bring her, bridally attired, by boat to the main bay, there to
glide in past the grotto and step ashore, with luck dry-shod,
at the foot of the road to the pinnacled monastery. However,
Sunday's rain gave way to a *maistro* wind . . . and a sea
voyage in a small boat was impossible. The bride had to
walk down under the olive trees and pick her way along a
wave-beaten shore to reach her car. The monastery court
was full of wind and sunlight and the pattern of sharp
shadows on fresh whitewash. Far below, the dark blue sea
was edged with foam and flung spray high towards us. Six
sucking pigs twirled on the spits. Costumed girls danced to
a fiddler's tunes. It was late afternoon before we dispersed,
the abbot vanishing into his quarters with the last little pig
under his arm.

NEIL MACVICAR, *A HEART'S ODYSSEY*

The Ceremony was very imposing, and fine and simple,
and I think *ought* to make an everlasting impression on
every one who promises at the altar to *keep* what he or
she promises. Dearest Albert repeated everything very
distinctly. I felt so happy when the ring was put on, and by

Albert. As soon as the Service was over, the procession returned as it came, with the exception that my beloved Albert led me out. The applause was very great, in the Colour Court as we came through; Lord Melbourne, good man, was very much affected during the Ceremony and at the applause. We all returned to the Throne-room, where the Signing of the Register took place; it was first signed by the Archbishop, then by Albert and me, and all the Royal Family, and by: the Lord Chancellor, the Lord President, the Lord Privy Seal, the Duke of Norfolk (as Earl Marshal), the Archbishop of York, and Lord Melbourne. We then went into the Closet, and the Royal Family waited with me there till the ladies had got into their carriages. I gave all the Train-bearers as a brooch a small eagle of turquoise. I then returned to Buckingham Palace alone with Albert; they cheered us really most warmly and heartily; the crowd was immense; and the Hall at Buckingham Palace was full of people; they cheered us again and again. The great Drawing-room and Throne-room were full of people of rank, and numbers of children were there. Lord Melbourne and Lord Clarendon, who had arrived, stood at the door of the Throne-room as we came in. I went and sat on the sofa in my dressing-room with Albert; and we talked together there from 10 m. to 2 till 20 m. p. 2. Then we went downstairs where all the Company was assembled and went into the dining-room – dearest Albert leading me in, and my Train being borne by 3 Pages, Cowell, little Wemyss, and dear little Byng. I sat between dearest Albert and the Duke of Sussex. My health and dearest Albert's were drunk. The Duke was very kind and civil. Albert and I drank a glass of wine with Lord Melbourne, who seemed much affected by the whole. I talked to all after the breakfast, and to Lord Melbourne, whose fine coat I praised . . . I went upstairs and undressed and put on a white silk gown trimmed with swansdown, and a bonnet with orange flowers. Albert went downstairs and undressed. At 20 m. to 4 Lord Melbourne came to me and stayed with me till 10 m. to 4. I shook hands with him and he kissed my hand. Talked of how well everything went off. 'Nothing could have gone off better,' he said, and of the people being in such good humour and having also received him well; of my receiving the Addresses from the House of Lords and Commons; of his coming down to Windsor in time for dinner, begged him not to go to the party; he was a little tired; I would let him know when we arrived; pressed his hand once more, and he said, 'God Bless you, Ma'am,' most kindly, and with such a kind look. Dearest Albert came up and fetched me downstairs where we took leave of Mamma and drove off at near 4; I and Albert alone.

QUEEN VICTORIA, 10 FEBRUARY 1840

John Milton, the great seventeenth-century English poet, in his *The Doctrine and Discipline of Divorce*, defines God's gift of marriage, and concludes that its 'chiefest and noblest' purpose is a 'happy conversation', by which is meant the living together in companionship of the couple and also the couple's relations with society. Milton's conclusion echoes that reached by many married people today, who believe the importance of communication to be a key factor in the making or breaking of the relationship:

And what his chief end was of creating woman to be joined with man, his own instituting words declare, and are infallible to inform us what is marriage and what is no marriage: unless we can think them set there to no purpose: 'It is not good', saith he, 'that man should be alone: I will make him a help meet for him.' From which words so plain, less cannot be concluded, nor is by any learned Interpreter, than that in God's intention a meet and happy conversation is the chiefest and the noblest end of marriage.

JOHN MILTON

Marriage, being a divine ordinance and a solemn engagement for the term of life, is of great importance to our peace and well-being in this world, and may prove of no small consequence respecting our state in that which is to come. It was designed for the mutual assistance and comfort of both sexes, that they might be meet-helps to each other, both in spirituals and temporals, and that their endeavours might be united for the pious and proper education of their children . . . May it never be inconsiderably entered into, upon motives inconsistent with the evident intention of that unerring Wisdom by which it was primarily ordained. Marriage implies union and concurrence, as well in spiritual as in temporal concerns.

SOCIETY OF FRIENDS, 1883

He thought of tomorrow, with the gay walk to the church, the walk back, the homely tea at Upper Leasowes, the loving comprehension that meant home for him. For it seemed to him that there was nothing about his thoughts unknown to his father; nothing about his hopes and fears with which Deborah did not sympathize; nothing about his bodily welfare that his mother did not forestall. All these emotions were quite dim and unexpressed; but they were none the less real to him. Then he thought how, when the rooks began to go home and the shadows to steal out of the hollows, and the first star sat like a bird on one arm of the devil's Chair, he would cease to be only 'the lad', and 'our Joe', and 'owd Joe of Upper Leasurs'. He would be a woman's all in all, and on his strength of hand and clearness of eye would depend two fates – perhaps many fates. They would walk down the path, 'just ordinary', they would come to the village, pass beyond it, pass the wicket. He would shut the door.

MARY WEBB

At the wedding of Ruby and Ernest, as described by Mary Webb in *The House in Dormer Forest*, material concerns, laced with carping comment, loom large:

> It was time to dress, and then, before she had half finished, there were the carriages – lent for the occasion by various neighbours – and there was Ruby with her veil half on and a very red face refusing to go downstairs unless she could have a definite promise from Ernest as to her dress allowance. Ruby was no weakling, and she seized the strategic hour. So Ernest had to be fetched from the drawing-room, where, before the greenish mirror, he was practising the saying of – 'I will' – soft, loud, modulated, mellifluous, gentle, virile, stentorian. He tried in all ways, and had almost decided upon stentorian, when in came Peter, very sulky, saying: 'The little fool says you're to promise a dress allowance or she'll chuck it.' Poor Ernest felt that perhaps 'modulated' would be best. He went up.
>
> 'Dear Ruby,' he said, 'such thoughts must not trouble us in this solemn hour. Nay, they shall not.'
>
> 'Fix it!' cried Ruby dramatically. 'Fix it, or no wedding!'
>
> 'She seems unstrung; she *is* unstrung,' said Ernest.
>
> 'Obstinate!' said her mother. 'Obstinate as a mule.'
>
> 'A mule – a mule!' sang grandmother.
>
> 'The price of a good woman is above rubies,' said Ernest helplessly.
>
> 'Fix it!' cried his bride.
>
> So fixed it was. But Ernest was so much disheartened that he could scarcely remember whether, after all, it was

to be stentorian or mellifluous. Everything, however, went well in church. Mr Mallow sang 'Oh, that I had the wings of a dove, for then would I flee away'. This was always a serious strain on Sarah's allegiance to Enoch. On the way back to the house Catherine remarked – 'He sings that same thing at every festival, and every time he sings it louder.'

'And better,' said Amber, for though Mr Mallow amused her, she did not like Catherine's bitter humour.

'And every time he sings it he is fatter, and his dream more impossible,' finished Catherine.

MARY WEBB

My parents have been divorced for a long time. They don't talk to each other unless they absolutely have to and for that reason I'd always dreaded organising my wedding.

Our reception took place at my father's house, so my stepmother took over most of the arrangements. But my mother was very gracious about it. There was only one occasion when she said it didn't really feel like her daughter's wedding.

My father caused me the most worry. He wanted my stepmother to be on the invitation as hostess and we had a big row about it. I really put my foot down, as Mum would have felt even more excluded. At one point I said I'd rather forget the whole thing and get married in a register office. Finally my stepmother said, 'If it's going to cause this much aggro, I don't want to be on the invitation,' and my father backed down.

On the day, though, it was OK; they all really enjoyed themselves and my parents were perfectly polite to one another. And we didn't have a sit-down reception, so I didn't have to agonise about the top-table seating-plan.

CHRISSIE GRAHAM, QUOTED IN BRIDES AND SETTING UP HOME,
JULY/AUGUST 1995

The woman was not made out of Adam's head, to rule over him, nor out of his feet to be trampled upon by him, but out of his side to be equal with him, under his arm to be protected, and near his heart to be beloved.

MATTHEW HENRY

Sacred, blithesome, undenied,
With benisons from East and West,
And salutations North and South,
Through me indeed to-day a million hearts and hands,
Wafting a million loves, a million soul-felt prayers;
 – Tender and true remain the arm that shields thee!
Fair winds always fill the ship's sails that sail thee!
Clear sun by day, and light stars at night, beam on thee!
Dear girl – through me the ancient privilege too,
For the New world, through me, the old, old wedding
    greeting:
O youth and health! O sweet Missouri rose! O bonny
    bride!
Yield thy red cheeks, thy lips, to-day,
Unto a Nation's loving kiss.

WALT WHITMAN

Ye gentle birds, the world's fair ornament,
And heaven's glory, whom this happy hour
Doth lead unto your lover's blissful bower,
Joy may you have and gentle heart's content
Of your love's couplement:
And let fair Venus, that is queen of love,
With her heart-quelling son upon you smile,
Whose smile they say, hath virtue to remove
All love's dislike, and friendship's faulty guile
For ever to assoil.

Let endless peace your steadfast hearts accord,
And blessèd plenty wait upon your board,
And let your bed with pleasures chaste abound,
That fruitful issue may to you afford,
Which may your foes confound,
And make your joys redound,
Upon your bridal day, which is not long:
   Sweet Thames run softly, till I end my song.

EDMUND SPENSER

line 7: 'Venus' heart-quelling son' is Cupid

Think of a wedding and, depending on what faith you are, it's odds on that your thoughts will turn to a fairytale church, a beautiful synagogue or a mystical mosque. It may be the first time you've thought about your love for each other in terms of religion and, let's face it, unless you met at a church social, lust rather than liturgy was probably what drew you together.

So, if when you decide to marry, you and your partner's (not to mention your respective families') religious differences become an issue, it may be all the more surprising. If you're a blissfully happy, multi-denominational couple, both cheerfully atheist or two committed Christians, you're lucky – these really are marriages made in heaven. But, spare a thought for less religiously-compatible couples, when they decide to have and to hold till death do them part, they may be entering a veritable minefield. The first hurdle to get over is deciding where to have the ceremony . . .

Religion is not like nationality; you cannot hold the spiritual equivalent of two passports, choosing which to use as the occasion demands. Two wedding ceremonies, one in each partner's church or temple may seem like the perfect solution, but rarely is it allowed to happen.

'Every door seemed to close in our faces,' remembers

Jackie, a Chilean-born Catholic interior designer married to Russell, a Jewish lawyer. 'We wanted to marry in a sacred place, although neither of us wanted or expected the other to convert. I spent months walking London's streets looking for a church which was prepared to marry us. The uncertainty put a huge strain on our relationship.' Russell takes up the story, 'Eventually, I was introduced to the vicar at St Lawrence Jewry in the City who, at last, made us incredibly welcome and we agreed a suitable service.'

Fortunately, both Jackie and Russell's parents were extremely supportive. 'They rated our happiness and health as far more important than religious dogma,' says Jackie, adding that the fact that her Catholic upbringing and Russell's Jewish background shared a great emphasis on really close family ties and this certainly helped overcome their religious differences and accelerated their acceptance within each other's families . . .

'A lot depends on the nature of your parental relationship – if you have close family bonds, it often follows that religion figures more prominently in your priorities,' suggests psychotherapist Christine Campbell, 'but, what you must honestly establish is the inner strength of your partner's religious belief. Ultimately, this should be far more decisive than the sentiments of your in laws-to-be' . . .

The ultimate diplomatic and spiritual compromise must surely be to both embrace a new and shared religious belief, a choice which Jewish-born journalist Sarah and Church of England barrister Hugh are convinced has enriched their marriage. 'We became interested in Quakerism through mutual friends and realised that it provided an ideal solution to our shared need for a non-denominational faith. Our unstructured marriage ceremony (there were no formal hymns or prayers) also seemed to make it easier for our relations to accept our decision.'

So, it would seem that although the path of true love rarely runs smooth, especially when it comes to partners with different faiths, there are ways to ensure that your marriage still remains a happy occasion. After all, it's not the ceremony itself which makes a successful marriage, it's your life together which is the real test. Marrying someone 'suitable' to keep your family happy or adopting a faith just to smooth things over is always a risky decision. It's always sensible to try to talk to family and friends about whatever decision you come to, but remember, it's your day and your life and you have to live it as you see fit.

SUDDI PIGGOT, *WEDDING AND HOME*,
OCTOBER/NOVEMBER 1994

Iris Murdoch on her first love, her husband of forty years, John Bayley, in the *Daily Mail*, 17 August 1996,

Bicycles do seem to have produced a certain amount of romance in our case, because we got off our bikes overnight on the way back from a friend's dinner party, and he kissed me for the first time. Our affair blossomed a bit then, but I still had absolutely no idea of marrying him or, indeed, anyone else, although he did suggest the idea in a rather diffident way.

His name was John Bayley, and he was just beginning to be an English literature tutor in another college. He was also writing a novel, an idea suggested by the wife of his former professor, and I was writing one too, so we talked a lot about that.

Our novels – first ones to be published for both of us – came out about the same time. (After a long interval devoted to academic work he has just written his fourth . . . My last one, *Jackson's Dilemma*, is I think my 26th.)

All that sounds very sober and like a literary friendship. But as time passed I realised that I was falling in love with him, and that he was my first love.

We got married two years later in 1956 at the Oxford register office. Not much celebration, though we did have a modest party at John's college with some very old champagne which the butler sold him cheap.

I still remember it, dark gold, not much fizz but delicious. I was still very much in love, although there was not much 'first' about it by that time.

Lynne Wallis, in the *Independent* 9 June 1997, described a humanist wedding which she found, as well as being fun, to be deeply moving:

> As atheists, the couple chose to have a humanist ceremony first, backed up by a register office the following weekend, more to keep their families happy than for any need they felt to legalise their vows.
>
> They hired a huge 14th-century country house in Sussex for their wedding weekend. Such opulence certainly hadn't been part of my idea of an 'alternative' wedding. The house slept 20 and came with pool, tennis courts, sauna and fabulously well kept grounds. The bride and groom welcomed their 80 or so guests at the door, she in a stunning blue satin, full-length, boned-bodiced dress with a net wrap around her shoulders; he in a trendy wool suit and clogs.
>
> The crowd was ushered through to an elegant drawing room for the ceremony while the bride and groom escaped for a few minutes to prepare themselves for their big moment. Grannies, parents and elderly aunts sat at the front in comfy sofas and armchairs, while remaining guests stood in this now rather full room. The scent of lilies wafted in from the hall and there wasn't a sound as the bride and

groom walked in and sat down, facing their guests, in two high-backed wooden fairy-tale chairs, like the King and Queen of Hearts, ready to vow their love for each other. It was such an emotionally loaded moment that clapping them seemed appropriate, so we did. I'd imagined some dreary, earnest types dressed down for the occasion in defiance of tradition, rather than up. Instead, here was a room full of colour, sparkle and excited anticipation, with no sombre priest, or po-faced organist to dampen the mood.

The couple could have arranged for a 'celebrant' from the Humanist Society to perform their ceremony. Instead, they opted for one of the groom's two best men, who explained what the ceremony entailed and proceeded expertly to 'MC' it. The bride had a six-strong coven of best women – she had so many close female friends that she'd felt unable to pick a 'best' one.

Friends each read some quotations chosen by the bride, from Jane Austen to the 10th-century poet Frau Ava. The last two, love poems, moved the groom almost to tears, which of course started the whole room off. There were speeches from the bride's mother and father, blessings, asked of grandparents and willingly given ('we've only been waiting for four years!') and finally the couple's vows, written by themselves. They promised to look after each other and love each other in the future, whatever that might hold, then exchanged simple gold bracelets and kissed.

Seeing their faces as they took their vows made the whole thing more meaningful, for me, than anything else could have, and it made me question the sense of church weddings, where the only person to see the important bit close up is someone the couple possibly met only a few days before, at rehearsals. Here, there wasn't a dry eye in the house. OK, God was out of the picture, and so for the moment was the law, but these two now regarded themselves as husband and wife, fully committed to their relationship for the future.

Married Life

Then Almitra spoke again and said, And what of Marriage, master?

And he answered saying:

You were born together, and together you shall be for evermore.

You shall be together when the white wings of death scatter your days.

Aye, you shall be together even in the silent memory of God.

But let there be spaces in your togetherness.

And let the winds of the heavens dance between you.

Love one another, but make not a bond of love:

Let it rather be a moving sea between the shores of your souls.

Fill each other's cup but drink not from one cup.

Give one another of your bread but eat not from the same loaf.

Sing and dance together and be joyous, but let each one of you be alone,

Even as the strings of a lute are alone though they quiver with the same music.

Give your hearts, but not into each other's keeping.

For only the hand of Life can contain your hearts.

And stand together yet not too near together:

For the pillars of the temple stand,

And the oak tree and the cypress grow not in each other's shadow.

KAHLIL GIBRAN, *THE PROPHET*

William Penn, a Quaker writing in 1693, offers these recommendations for marriage:

> Between a man and his wife nothing ought to rule but love . . .
> As love ought to bring them together, so it is the best way to keep them well together.
>
> A husband and wife that love and value one another show their children that they should do so too.
> Others visibly lose their authority in their families by their contempt of one another; and teach their children to be unnatural by their own examples.
>
> Let not enjoyment lessen, but augment, affection; it being the basest of passions to like when we have not, what we slight when we possess.
>
> Here it is we ought to search out our pleasure, where the field is large and full of variety, and of an enduring nature; sickness, poverty, or disgrace being not able to shake it, because it is not under the moving influences of worldly contingencies.
>
> Nothing can be more entire and without reserve; nothing more zealous, affectionate and sincere; nothing more contented and constant than such a couple, nor no greater temporal felicity than to be one of them.

Barrow Cadbury, another Quaker, writing in 1933, has this to say to the newly-married couple:

> Start out together on a fifty-fifty basis, each sharing with the other, and thereby doubly enriching both. Recognise the equality of the service each performs, even though the work differs . . . The wider your interests outside your

regular occupation, the more companionship you will enjoy together, and the happier and more fruitful life will be. After all, if two people are going to live together for thirty, forty, or sixty years they must have interesting things to talk about, or they will get cruelly on one another's nerves. It needs a real effort to cultivate new interests, but the effort is well repaid.

Cadbury's observations are as acute as they are profound. It is vital in marriage that the one should recognise equality in the service performed by the other: if one goes out to work and the other keeps house, these are equal functions. The one who earns a pay cheque should never demean the one who shops and gets the dinner ready. Cadbury is good on shared interests – whether held in common or of mutual concern – and is not afraid to acknowledge that without them a couple may grate painfully together.

The animals teach us to trust ourselves; what we are to trust is not the self-confident, self-directed part of ourselves, the 'plain man' who knows what is what and how to get on, but the whole of ourselves. And the greater part of this whole we can only become acquainted with after many years, and only then by the patient surrender of pride in a willingness to live with the shabby and unpredictable in ourselves, without trying to pretend it isn't there. It can destroy us if we ignore it, but if we acknowledge it it becomes our guide. It is itself changed, no longer hidden but a known part of ourselves.

ROSEMARY HAUGHTON, *TALES FROM ETERNITY*

Elizabeth Montagu writes to Gilbert West, 1754, on the occasion of Mr Pitt becoming engaged to Lady Hester Grenville, Gilbert West's cousin:

I believe Lady Hester Grenville is very good-humoured, which is the principal article in the happiness of the Marriage State. Beauty soon grows familiar to the lover, wit may be pernicious, and many brilliant qualities troublesome; but a companion of gentle disposition softens cares and lightens sorrows. The sober matches made on reflection, are often happier than those made by sudden and violent passion.

ELIZABETH MONTAGU

Some of the popular expressions about marriage imply a belief that it is like a game of chance or a lottery, with one prize to a thousand blanks. That is a cynical view of marriage, like the rather profane saying that if matches are made in heaven, they are dipped in the other place! Those who are unequally yoked will believe this adage to be true, but those between whom there is harmony of physical and mental conditions will consider marriage to be a heaven upon earth; but this can only be attained by a proper adaptation of husband to wife.

An imperative duty which married people owe to each other is fidelity to the marriage vow. This is a duty so sacred that the least suspicion cast on it will throw a blight over their happiness. By fidelity we mean not only the avoidance of gross and open outrage of the conjugal covenant, but flirtations and all acts which give any occasion for jealousy. Beware of trifling with the vows you made at the altar, and let each join in chorus and say:-

Through shade and sunshine, ever still the same,
Dreaming of thee:
I would not, could not, change, whate'er betide,
But constant be.

To cultivate a cheerful disposition is another desirable feature of married life. All persons are not equally endowed with a hopeful spirit, but the model husband and wife should cultivate cheerfulness.

LOVE, COURTSHIP AND MARRIAGE

Though Mrs Porter was double the age of Johnson, and her person and manner, as described to me by the late Mr Garrick, were by no means pleasing to others, she must have had a superiority of understanding and talents, as she certainly inspired him with a more than ordinary passion; and she having signified her willingness to accept of his hand, he went to Lichfield to ask his mother's consent to the marriage, which he could not but be conscious was a very imprudent scheme, both on account of their disparity of years, and her want of fortune. But Mrs Johnson knew too well the ardour of her son's temper, and was too tender a parent to oppose his inclinations.

I have had from my illustrious friend the following curious account of their journey to church upon the nuptial morn:

9th July:- 'Sir, she had read the old romances, and had got into her head the fantastical notion that a woman of spirit should use her lover like a dog. So, Sir, at first she told me that I rode too fast, and she could not keep up with me; and, when I rode a little slower, she passed me, and complained that I lagged behind. I was not to be made the slave of caprice; and I resolved to begin as I meant to end. I therefore pushed on briskly, till I was fairly out of her sight. The road lay between two hedges, so I was sure she could not miss it; and I contrived that she should soon come up with me. When she did, I observed her to be in tears.'

This, it must be allowed, was a singular beginning of connubial felicity; but there is no doubt that Johnson, though he thus shewed a manly firmness, proved a most affectionate and indulgent husband.

JAMES BOSWELL, *THE LIFE OF SAMUEL JOHNSON*

Marriage may be called a recipe for conflict, and cannot be without disputes and quarrels. Here is a spirited, good-natured and humorous exchange of letters, March/April 1776, between Abigail Adams and her husband John Adams, one of the founding fathers of the United States of America, who became its second president the following year.

She wrote to him:

... in the new Code of Laws which I suppose it will be necessary for you to make I desire you would Remember the Ladies, and be more generous and favourable to them than your ancestors. Do not put such unlimited power into the hands of the Husbands. Remember all Men would be tyrants if they could. If particular care and attention is not paid to the Ladies we are determined to foment a Rebellion, and will not hold ourselves bound by any Laws in which we have no voice, or Representation.

That your Sex are Naturally Tyrannical is a Truth so thoroughly established as to admit of no dispute, but such of you as wish to be happy willingly give up the harsh title of Master for the more tender and endearing one of Friend.

He replied:

As to your extraordinary Code of Laws, I cannot but laugh. We have been told that our Struggle has loosened the bands of Government every where. That Children and Apprentices were disobedient – that schools and Colledges were grown turbulent – that Indians slighted their Guardians and Negroes grew insolent to their Masters. But your Letter was the first Intimation that another Tribe more numerous and more powerfull than all the rest were grown discontented. – This is rather too coarse a Compliment but you are so saucy, I won't blot it out.

An anonymous writer of the Victorian period, in *Love, Courtship and Marriage*, gives the following prescription:

Let the rebuke be preceded by a kiss.
Do not require a request to be repeated.
Never should both be angry at the same time.
Never neglect the other, for all the world beside.
Let the angry word be answered only with a kiss.
Bestow your warmest sympathies in each other's trials.
Never make a remark calculated to bring ridicule upon the
    other.
Make your criticism in the most loving manner possible.
Make no display of the sacrifices you make for each other.
Never reproach the other for an error which was done with
    a good motive and with the best judgment at the time.
Always leave home with a tender good-bye and loving
    words.

As a mantra for marriage, this can hardly be bettered. The advice is practical, and is relevant day by day.

Just as your first date and your first kiss were pivotal points in your relationship, so too is your first marital argument. First arguments can be particularly upsetting because along with the quarrel itself, you also have to deal with the realisation that you and your partner do not agree on absolutely everything, as you might have previously believed. The secret with your first and any subsequent quarrels you have is to turn them to your advantage by using them to establish a climate of strong and trusting communication, and to learn more about your partner. How you deal with the first problems that arise in your marriage will set the tone for what takes place in the years to come, so approach your first disagreements with great thought and care . . .

Often, couples will quarrel because one or other of them is under stress or feeling uncertain about an area of their lives, and newly-weds are particularly vulnerable. After you marry, you have to find the emotional balance between maintaining your individuality . . . and being part of a couple. You also acquire another family overnight, and the pressures and expectations that accompany the possibility of a family of your own. In addition, if you did not live with your spouse before you were married, you have to adjust to having them around 24 hours a day. (Even though all you ever wanted was to be together, having this particular wish come true can be something of a shock – and those little habits of your partner's that were so endearing before can take on lives of their own when you have to live with them.) . . .

One very damaging myth surrounding marriage is that couples are supposed to know what each other is thinking and feeling without being told. In reality, most people find it very difficult to guess accurately what another person is feeling. If something is bothering you, don't assume your partner will know what it is automatically. Instead of walking around with a long face and letting your resentment build up, sit your partner down, tell them the problem, and you will have taken positive steps towards a resolution . . .

If there are any areas in your marriage that are of particular contention, one strategy is to address them before they address you . . .

It's a good idea to accept the fact that you will argue at some point in your marriage. Although it might be earth-shattering at the time, one argument (or even many) does not sound the death knell for a relationship. Arguments are all part and parcel of the learning curve in your relations – why not regard them as the few unsatisfactory apples in an otherwise flourishing orchard?

It can be difficult to get your feet back on the ground after all the excitement of your wedding day, but it is important that you don't nurture unrealistic expectations of your marriage or your partner . . . Realise and appreciate the limitations and strengths of yourself and your partner and use them to your mutual advantage – make sure that if you and your partner do argue, it's over a valid issue, not a self-created one. Value your spouse for the warm and loving person that he or she is, keep your sense of humour and perspective, and with perseverance, patience and a realistic attitude, you can resolve your problems and have the long, strong and healthy marriage that you both deserve.

JENNI JAMES IN *BRIDES AND SETTING UP HOME*,
MAY/JUNE 1996

Have your good healthy quarrels, even forget that you are decently brought up people, and shout at each other if it helps, but once the quarrel is over, well, ring down the curtain on that particular disagreement. While it is in progress, fight fairly, listen to what the other person has to say, don't use weapons which are unworthy of you, don't use phrases which have nothing to do with the point at issue and are only voiced to wound and sting. And, don't nurse grievances or let the sun go down on your anger.

And blessings on the falling out,
That all the more endears,
When we fall out with those we love,
And kiss again with tears.

Very pleasant poetry no doubt, but don't 'fall out with those you love' too often, or you may find that even the 'kissing again with tears' loses its efficacy, and becomes a mere form, and that its actual meaning has worn so thin that it is practically invisible.

. . . once a quarrel is over – forget it. Don't let it rankle, don't nurse grievances, try and blot the whole thing from your memory. I remember when I first read Louisa Alcott's *Little Women*, even as quite a small child being tremendously struck with Mrs March's admonition, 'Never let the sun go down on your anger'. It has not been possible to completely wipe out all one's dislikes and anger against some person who has hurt or injured us, but for the people with whom we live, who will sleep under the same roof as we do, it is surely possible in 90 per cent of the quarrels which happen to 'make it up' before you close your eyes for the night. Probably the quarrel all started about nothing, and even if it were something really serious – unless it should unhappily be something cataclysmic, something which has shaken your world to its very foundations – make it up and let tomorrow's sun rise on a determination to 'make a go of things'.

NAOMI JACOB, *ME – THINKING THINGS OVER*

Samuel Pepys in his famous *Diary* affords a good example of a grievance resolved before the morrow:

Jan. 12, 1668–9. This evening I observed my wife mighty dull, and I myself was not mighty fond, because of some hard words she did give me at noon, out of a jealousy at my being abroad this morning, which, God knows, it was upon the business of the Office unexpectedly; but I to bed, not thinking but she would come after me.

She did come to bed eventually, but not before teasing Pepys with a bedpan filled with red-hot coals, and they lay and talked happily together until they slept.

A good marriage depends on developing a clear picture of our own lives, a difficult and painful process for many of us. Too often we pretend that what passes as 'good enough' is actually good – telling ourselves we're satisfied when we're not, that we love someone we don't, or that someone loves us when we know deep down inside that he doesn't. We sometimes marry because we want to be safe, cared for, or because we don't want to be regarded as unable to marry. We talk ourselves into relationships that are like an inoculation against life rather than part of it. This sort of marriage might keep bad things away, but it's just as likely to keep good things away.

REGINA BARRECA, *PERFECT HUSBANDS (AND OTHER FAIRY TALES)*

H. G. Wells, in his novel *Marriage*, addresses the matter of communication between spouses:

Talking one's relations over isn't particularly easy between husband and wife at any time; we are none of us so sure of one another as to risk loose phrases or make experiments in expression in matters so vital; there is inevitably an excessive caution on the one hand and an abnormal sensitiveness to things and implications on the other . . . Moreover, when two people are continuously together, it is amazingly hard to know when and where to begin; where intercourse is unbroken it is a matter of routine being constantly interrupted. You cannot broach these broad personalities while you are getting up in the morning, or when you meet again after a multitude of small events at tea, or in the evening when one is rather tired and trivial after the work of the day.

Here, potential moments of crisis in a marriage are pinpointed:

At any point a wonderful spouse can stop being one; adultery usually eclipses years of fidelity, for example, or a broken rib eclipses years of non-violence. Words, too, can be indelible; once said, they can alter the atmosphere in a room as profoundly as tear gas – and often with the same result. One destructive act has the potential to change the very definition of the relationship. A person can go from being a good husband – or wife – to a bad one in the space of five minutes. The nineteenth-century philosopher Kierkegaard pointed out that romantic love can very well be represented in the moment, but conjugal love cannot, because an ideal husband is not one who is such once in his life, but one who every day is such.

REGINA BARRECA, *PERFECT HUSBANDS* (*AND OTHER FAIRY TALES*)

This may seem obvious, but do marry someone you like. Love is a devilish cocktail of chemicals and conditioning and your hormones are in no condition to sift judgement from pleasure. If at the engagement party Mr/Ms Right is cursory to your parents and patronising to your friends and monopolises you at the expense of your personal growth, then they are Mr/Ms Seriously Wrong. There are thousands of women out there, and undoubtedly some men, who honestly believed at the altar that they, and only they, could alter the loved one by the application of tact and understanding. This is known as a mercy marriage and, since it exhibits both arrogance and lack of self-esteem, refuges are full of the casualties of such unions.

Finally, let me confess to you bonny and blushing brides and grooms that for 21 years I have been asked *ad nauseam*, what is the secret of keeping a marriage contentedly bobbing along, particularly in a show-biz setting for so long. It's like saying to the winner of the lottery, 'How did you do it?' There's no recipe, no magic ingredient, although humour helps. A little pride in each other, a lot of patience, your own front door, the odd shared interest, a healthy ability to argue without sulking, and a healthy but not overly-lecherous libido . . . and if you're planning on having children, don't marry one.

MAUREEN LIPMAN IN *BRIDES AND SETTING UP HOME*,
JULY/AUGUST 1995

William Cobbett, in his *Advice to Young Men and Women*, has this to say (he is addressing a young man, but he might just as well have been addressing a young woman):

> You should never forget that marriage, which is a state that every young person ought to have in view, is a thing to last for life; and that, generally speaking, it is to make life happy or miserable . . . Marriage brings numerous cares, which are amply compensated by the more numerous delights which are their companions. But to have the delights, as well as the cares, the choice of the partner must be fortunate. Say fortunate; for, after all, love, real love, impassioned affection, is an ingredient so absolutely necessary, that no perfect reliance can be placed on the judgement. Yet the judgement may do something; reason

may have some influence; and, therefore, I here offer you my advice with regard to the exercise of that reason.

The things which you ought to desire . . . are, 1. Chastity; 2. Sobriety; 3. Industry; 4. Frugality; 5. Cleanliness; 6. Knowledge of domestic affairs; 7. Good temper; 8. Beauty.

The following words of warning may still be relevant:

May no right union be unduly delayed by overmuch carefulness as to a provision for the future. It would be far indeed from our desire to encourage a hasty and ill-advised procedure in this important matter; but we fear that, in the present day of increasing luxury and ease, there may have been a tendency, from considerations of mere worldly prudence, too long to defer unions which, with moderate views and simpler faith, might have been productive of mutual help and joy.

SOCIETY OF FRIENDS, 1869

When my boyfriend proposed, and I accepted, everyone thought we were mad. It was eight years ago, and I had just turned 20 and was two terms away from taking my finals.

When I appeared at Oxford wearing an engagement ring, I found myself the object of the sort of pity usually reserved for the most bedraggled animals at the zoo. What was I thinking of to tie myself down so young? Didn't I want a career? Didn't I want to play around a bit first? (This last often from drunken chaps with leering, hopeful eyes. Well, certainly not with you, thanks very much.)

Today, an intelligent girl is supposed to get her degree, find a job, share a flat, enjoy her freedom and then, *maybe*, get married. If she gets hitched too young, she is copping out, settling for a limited life and exchanging ambition for a dubious security that will probably end in divorce anyway.

But I was so determined that I got married – at 21 – anyway. And looking back, I'm amazed I had the courage – for, in its own way, marrying early these days flouts convention as much as remaining single did in Jane Austen's time.

Yet marrying young does not have to be limiting. Marital vows do not include any references to vacuuming, dusting or bypassing ambition. They are founded on a promise to love and cherish. If your idea of this is receiving a housekeeping allowance every month, fine. If it's being encouraged to pursue your ambition as energetically as you can, then that's good too.

My own ambition was to write a book. For nearly four months, I spent every spare moment working on it. I didn't have time to cook, see films or dust. So my husband made supper, went to the cinema with friends, read chapters as they were printed out and never once complained or said: 'Oh God, you're so boring these days.'

Would a boyfriend have been so understanding? Would I have kept at it if I'd been living on my own? I don't think so. The thing about marriage is that it's for ever. You can take out four months without feeling that the relationship is going to crumble. You can think long term; you have the freedom to gamble.

For me, the gamble paid off . . .

Far from limiting me, marriage enabled me to pursue my goal. And it is a reciprocal arrangement. When my husband announced he was chucking in his job with the BBC Singers to go freelance, I was the one doing the supporting, the encouraging and the cooking, while he raced to auditions and learnt new music (in one instance, learning the part of Figaro in a single week, with me bashing it out on the piano).

It was for this kind of partnership that we got married in the first place. We didn't do it simply to express our love, or to have a good party. We are a team; that's why I took his name – another detail my peers find shocking. An author in her twenties, using her married name? It's old-fashioned, it's anti-feminist, it's just not what young girls *do* these days.

Neither are we supposed to have children when young. But getting married doesn't necessarily entail having children immediately. I've had six years of marriage and six months of having a baby. Motherhood is joyous, but I am glad that we were able to have several years together without children.

I'm not against staying single; I just don't believe it is better or more advisable than marrying at an unfashionably early age. For us, marriage hasn't been about security, or sets of china from John Lewis. It has been our springboard. We've had more fun, been more creative and felt more confident *because* we married young.

MADELEINE WICKHAM 'IT'S GREAT TO GET MARRIED AT 21', IN
DAILY TELEGRAPH, 21 APRIL 1997

A gentleman who had been very unhappy in marriage, married immediately after his wife died: Johnson said that it was the triumph of hope over experience.

JAMES BOSWELL

Marriage is the best state for a man in general; and every man is a worse man, in proportion as he is unfit for the married state.

SAMUEL JOHNSON

Nothing is to me more distasteful than that entire complacency and satisfaction which beam in the countenances of a new-married couple.

CHARLES LAMB, *A BACHELOR'S COMPLAINT OF MARRIED
PEOPLE*

Marriage is like a cage; one sees the birds outside desperate to get in, and those inside equally desperate to get out.

MICHEL DE MONTAIGNE, *ESSAIS, III*

A married couple are well suited when both partners usually feel the need for a quarrel at the same time.

JEAN ROSTAND, *LE MARIAGE*

Never feel remorse for what you have thought about your wife; she has thought much worse things about you.

JEAN ROSTAND, *LE MARIAGE*

It takes two to make a marriage a success and only one a failure.

HERBERT SAMUEL, *A BOOK OF QUOTATIONS*

My definition of marriage . . . it resembles a pair of shears, so joined that they cannot be separated; often moving in opposite directions, yet always punishing anyone who comes between them.

SIDNEY SMITH, *MEMOIRS*

Each coming together of man and wife, even if they have been mated for many years, should be a fresh adventure; each winning should necessitate a fresh wooing.

MARIE STOPES, *MARRIED LOVE*

Marriage is a School and Exercise of Virtue; and though Marriage hath Cares, yet the Single Life hath Desires, which are more troublesome and more dangerous, and often end in Sin; while the Cares are but Instances of Duty, and Exercises of Piety; and therefore if Single Life hath more Privacy of Devotion, yet Marriage hath more Necessities and more Variety of it, and is an Exercise of more Graces.

Marriage is the proper Scene of Piety and Patience, of the Duty of Parents and the Charity of Relations; here Kindness is spread Abroad, and Love is united and made firm as a Centre; Marriage is the Nursery of Heaven ... Marriage ... hath in it the Labour of Love, and the Delicacies of Friendship, the Blessing of Society, and the Union of Hands and Hearts. It hath in it less of Beauty, but more of Safety than the Single Life; it hath more Care, but less Danger; it is more Merry, and more Sad; is fuller of Sorrows, and fuller of Joys; it lies under more Burdens, but is supported by all the Strengths of Love and Charity, and those Burdens are delightful.

JEREMY TAYLOR, *SERMONS: THE MARRIAGE RING*

One of the crucial problems of human society and human happiness lies in the question of how far marriage is a help or a hindrance to a mutual love and its continuance. One of the commonest reasons, apart from other human frailties, why it falls short of a perfection is that the promise *had* to be made, was kept with joy for a time and then broken, and not necessarily either light-headedly or light-heartedly. A broken promise may sometimes be repaired; and may then, if love managed the mending of it and supplied the cement, look almost as good as new ...

But in no circumstances can we remain at any extremity either of passion, happiness or misery. A love stagnant is a love in decay. It is living, or dying. In any shared life there is bound to be some conflict. To fight it out may prove more or less fatal to one of the contestants and grievous for both. Only compromise with the aid of its last two syllables can make peace. Love doesn't *make* peace. It gives it, as the flame even of a candle, of an intense, however narrow, activity, gives both light and heat.

WALTER DE LA MARE, *LOVE*

There are marriages of convenience; marriages intent on an heir, a housekeeper, or a home; on comfort or companionship; the outcome of pique or mere caprice. But 'the pang of all the partings gone', the supreme and overmastering desire of any two humans who are in love with one another is to be together and alone, in a shared and mutual solitude. That (in much) is what weddings are for. It is attained and safeguarded in marriage. How well and happily then should it be spoken of, how profound should be its appeal to our common humanity.

WALTER DE LA MARE, *Love*

Casual acquaintances, who in later years saw the husband and wife together, the former attracting a group of listeners, with his bright face, animated manner, and eager gesticulation; the latter, sitting quietly knitting . . . would perhaps have hardly guessed how much he really leant on her – in some ways, if not actually the stronger, certainly the calmer, character of the two. Her evenness of temper, her sterling every-day good sense and unselfish sympathy made her the ideal wife for a man like himself. Their married happiness was as near perfection as anything on this side of Eden could be.

CHRISTOPHER WORDSWORTH, BISHOP OF LINCOLN

I used to wonder in the old days, at the extraordinary alliances which I saw. A husband of vivid intellectual sympathies and a dull, homely wife; or a brilliant, artistic, sensitive woman, with a robust and comfortable mate. And yet such misfits often seemed the most contented combinations. One did not see that mutual love is often best sustained by an admiration for opposite qualities – that the brilliant husband could see the superficiality of his own flourishes, and repose gratefully upon his wife's sense and practical judgement, while the wife could unenvyingly admire a vividness which she could not understand. One forgot the necessary alternations of stimulus and restfulness, one overlooked the meaning of the whole affair. What matters most of all in life is mutual confidence, the sense of unity, not of idea and not even of aim, but of regard and hope. What makes many people miss happiness in life – and this is particularly true of intellectual people – is that they look too much for partnership in superficial things, and make the mistake of thinking that life means occupation and talk. Life is a much deeper and stronger thing than that; occupation is often nothing more than the channel in which it flows, while talk is but the breaking of bubbles on the surface of the stream.

A. C. BENSON, *ALONG THE ROAD*

When day dawned (for we did not sleep much) and I beheld the beautiful angelic face by my side, it was more than I can express! He does look so beautiful in his shirt only, with his beautiful throat seen. We got up at 1/4 p. 8. When I had laced I went to dearest Albert's room, and we breakfasted together. He had a black velvet jacket on, without any neckcloth on, and looked more beautiful than it is possible for me to say... At 12 I walked out with my precious Angel, all alone – so delightful, on the Terrace and new Walk, arm in arm! Eros our only companion. We talked a great deal together. We came home at one, and had luncheon soon after. Poor dear Albert felt sick and uncomfortable, and lay down in my room ... He looked so dear, lying there and dozing.

My dearest Albert put on my stockings for me. I went in and saw him shave; a great delight for me.

QUEEN VICTORIA, 11 AND 13 FEBRUARY 1840

Marriage

How do I love thee? Let me count the ways.
I love thee to the depth and breadth and height
My soul can reach, when feeling out of sight
For the end of Being and ideal Grace.
I love thee to the level of every day's
Most quiet need, by sun and candlelight.
I love thee freely, as men strive for Right;
I love thee purely, as they turn from Praise.
I love thee with the passion put to use
In my old griefs, and with my childhood's faith.
I love thee with a love I seemed to lose
With my lost saints – I love thee with the breath,
Smiles, tears, of all my life! – and, if God choose,
I shall but love thee better after death.

ELIZABETH BARRETT BROWNING

Whether in the years since then I have accomplished anything worth while or not, I have thoroughly enjoyed living.
Love is no stranger to me. My love affairs began in childhood and have been going on ever since in varying kinds
and with as many results. Love is good wherever it comes
from. I am married now, and I find that good too. Economic
freedom is good, and I still have it. But it seems to me that
in these days of rapidly increasing fair play between a man
and a woman neither economic dependence or independence makes much difference. It is the spirit of cooperation
that counts and enables two people to make adjustments
both inside and outside of their relationship.

ANON.

We that are sprung of distant whole
Of which we nothing know, nor need
To know perhaps, each one a soul
Planted as single as the seed

161

Weddings

Scattered from unseen Sowers' hands:
We too belong to different lands
Of colour, rhythm, tune and heart,
And star-like each is set apart
And bidden play his proper part.

The pillar poplar and the birch
Quiver delight yet never touch
Each other's mystic centres. Bruise
Their broken flowers, nothing ensues,
Though wandering perfumes sweet confuse.
Chalk, clay and sand scarcely commingle
Keeping their levels, and ourselves
Remain like books on different shelves
Companioned but forever single.

Yet star and star can sing together
And trees can bend in the autumn weather
Beneath a common tempest arching,
While men of different stamp and kind
Keep step for gladness in their marching
As mind, for love, keeps step with mind.
Thus men and women in their need
Turn and give hands, not taking heed
Of those peculiar symmetries
Wherein the ultimate sanction lies.
They can approach and gently take
Clear draughts of warmth which kindness lends,
And that sheer calm and peace which friends
Yield to each other from their eyes.

ROLF GARDINER

To my Dear and Loving Husband

>If ever two were one, then surely we.
>If ever man were loved by wife, then thee;
>If ever wife was happy in a man,
>Compare with me, ye women, if you can.
>I prize thy love more than whole mines of gold
>Or all the riches that the East doth hold.
>My love is such that rivers cannot quench,
>Nor ought but love from thee, give recompense.
>Thy love is such I can no way repay,
>The heavens reward thee manifold, I pray.
>Then while we live, in love let's so persever
>That when we live no more, we may live ever.

ANNE BRADSTREET

The date and provenance of the following frivolous verses, entitled *Crumbs of Comfort for the Single Ladies of Anywhere Affectionately Presented to Them by the Married Ladies of Somewhere*, are unknown; but the burden of the piece, that 'courtship is one thing and wedlock another', is a comment on the state of matrimony that could have provoked wry smiles at any time in the past five hundred years.

>We're married – we're married and find, O! ye fair
>Our Castles of happiness built but in air.
>They were guarded by Cupids who promised to stay,
>Yet on Hymen's arrival, the rogues fled away.
>Our stores of felicity are but a joke
>And the bright luck of Hymen has ended in smoke.
>
>'Tis true we no longer dread people who say
>Do look at that 'Old Maid' just over the way,
>But it's still more appalling for some one to sigh
>And remark 'how neglected is poor Mrs I'.
>That sweet Mrs A makes an excellent wife
>But her Husband's so cross she is weary of life . . .

Weddings

Silly things! we won't think that these lords of Creation
Who when single beheld us with such admiration
Who swear and who vow their existence depends
On a look – on a word – that they'd compass the ends
Of the World, to procure us a moment's repose,
Will as soon as we marry 'em turn up their nose
At our tears our entreaties and look on our grief
With a stoic philosophy passing belief . . .

There once was a time Mr — when you swore
My wishes should even – Pshaw, Madam, no more,
That nonsense is over, I've had time to cool,
Married men soon get tired of playing the fool;
I've just bought that hunter, those dogs, changed my gun
And must pay Snip the Tailor, that fellow's a Dun.
A little reflection I'm sure Mrs — ask
Would shew you 'tis selfish to ask now for cash,
But so thoughtless you are, as I've told you before
'Twould drive any man mad, exit slamming the door.

Oh! Sisters – dear Sisters, your liberty prize,
In true 'single blessedness' stay if you're wise.
Leading Asses by dozens can never compare
With the lectures you'd suffer if led by a Bear,
And how'er you may flatter yourselves or each other
You'll find Courtship is one thing and Wedlock another.

FROM ELEANOR PORTER & MARY ABBOTT, *YEOMEN OF THE COTSWOLDS*

Thomas Turner (1729–93) worked as a schoolmaster in East Hoathly, Sussex, where he later kept a general store. The passages that follow are from his diary.

This morn my wife and I had words about her going to Lewes tomorrow; Oh, what happiness must there be in the

164

married state, when there is a sincere regard on both sides, and each party truly satisfied with each other's merits! But it is impossible for tongue or pen to express the uneasiness that attends the contrary.

30 MARCH 1755

This is the day on which I was married and it is now three years since. Doubtless many have been the disputes which have happened between my wife and myself during the time, and many have been the afflictions which it has pleased God to lay upon us, and which we may have justly deserved by the many animosities and dissensions which have been continually fermented between us and our friends, from allmost the very day of our marriage; but I may now say with the holy Psalmist, 'It is good for us that we have been afflicted'; for, thanks be to God, we now begin to live happy; and I am thoroughly persuaded, if I know my own mind, that if I was single again, and at liberty to make another choice, I should do the same – I mean make her my wife who is so now.

15 OCTOBER 1756

Oh, how happy must that man be whose more than happy lot it is to whom an agreeable company for life doth fall – one in whom he sees and enjoys all that this world can give; to whom he can open the inmost recesses of his soul, and receive mutual and pleasing comfort to soothe those anxious and tumultuous thoughts that must arise in the breast of any man in trade! On the contrary, and I can speak from woful experience – how miserable must they be, where there is nothing else but matrimonial discord and domestic disquietude! How do these thoughts wrack my tumultuous breast, and chill the purple current in my veins! Oh, how are these delusive hopes and prospects of

happiness before marriage turned into briars and thorns!
But, as happiness is debarred me in this affair, I sincerely
wish it to all those that shall ever tye the Gordian knot. Oh
woman, ungrateful woman! thou that wast the last and most
compleatest of the creation, and designed by Almighty God
for a comfort and companion to mankind, to smooth and
make even the rough and uneven paths of life, are often, oh
too, too often, the very bane and destroyer of our felicity!
Thou not only takest away our happiness, but givest us, in
lieu thereof, trouble and vexation of spirit.

7 OCTOBER 1758

Thomas Turner was twice married. Here he is courting Molly
Hicks who became his second wife.

In the afternoon rode over to Chiddingly, to pay my
charmer, or intended wife, or sweetheart, or whatever other
name may be more proper, a visit at her father's, where I
drank tea, in company with their family and Miss Ann
Thatcher. I supped there on some rashers of bacon. It being
an excessive wet and windy night I had the opportunity,
sure I should say the pleasure, or perhaps some might say
the unspeakable happiness, to sit up with Molly Hicks, or
my charmer, all night. I came home at forty minutes past
five in the morning – I must not say fatigued; no, no, that
could not be it; it could be only a little sleepy for want of
rest. Well, to be sure, she is a most clever girl; but however,
to be serious in the affair, I certainly esteem the girl, and
think she appears worthy of my esteem.

18 MARCH 1765

After dinner I set out for Malling, to pay Molly Hicks, my
intended wife, a visit, with whom I intended to go to
church, but there was no afternoon service. I spent the

afternoon with a great deal of pleasure, it being very fine, pleasant weather, and my companion very agreeable. Now, perhaps, there may be many reports abroad in the world of my present intentions, some likely condemning my choice, others approving it; but as the world cannot judge the secret intentions of my mind, and I may therefore be censured, I will take the trouble to relate what really and truly are my intentions, and the only motive from which they spring (which may be some satisfaction to those who may happen to peruse my memoirs). First, I think marriage is a state agreeable to nature, reason and religion; I think it the duty of every Christian to serve God and perform his religious services in the most calm, serene, and composed manner, which, if it can be performed more so in the married state than in a single one, it must then be an indispensable duty . . .

As to my choice, I have only this to say: the girl, I believe, as far as I can discover, is a very industrious, sober woman and seemingly endued with prudence, and good nature, with a serious and sedate turn of mind. She comes of reputable parents, and may perhaps, one time or other, have some fortune. As to her person, I know it's plain (so is my own), but she is cleanly in her person, and dress, which I will say is something more than at first sight it may appear to be, towards happiness. She is, I think, a well-made woman. As to her education, I own it is not liberal; but she has good sense, and a desire to improve her mind, and has always behaved to me with the strictest honour and good manners – her behaviour being far from the affected formality of the prude, on the one hand; and on the other, of the foolish fondness too often found in the more light part of the sex. For myself, I have nothing else in view but to live in a more sober and regular manner, to perform my duty to God and man in a more suitable and religious manner, and, with the grace of the Supreme Being, to live happy in a sincere union with the partner of my bosom.

15 APRIL 1765

Marriage is to be taken seriously, but not always in grim earnest; its problems take perspective from fun, adventure and fulfilment, and joy and sorrow are mingled together. We rejoice in success, but we must also be glad that we can console each other in failure. 'With my body I thee worship' is to many a blessed phrase: but while some find a perfect physical relationship easily, others reach it the hard way, and it is not less precious for that. It is wonderful never to quarrel, but it means missing the dear delight of making it up. Children bring joy and grief; some will have none and will miss both the grief and the joy. For some, there is a monogamy so entire that no other love ever touches it; but others 'fall in love' time and time again, and must learn to make riches of their affection without destroying their marriages or their friends. Let us thank God for what we share, which enables us to understand; and for the infinite variety in which each marriage stands alone.

SOCIETY OF FRIENDS

The lady of the house is on her benders;
She's scrubbed and mopped until her knees are sore.
She rests a second as her husband enters,
Then says, 'Look out! Don't walk on my clean floor.'
He looks up at the slick flies on the ceiling
and shakes his head, and goes back through the door.

She holds her chuckling baby to her bosom
And says, 'My honey-pie, my sugar bun,
Does Mummy love her scrumptious little darling?
You're lovely, yes, you are, my precious one!'

But when the little perisher starts bawling
She says, 'For God's sake listen to your son.'

Sandbagged by sleep at last the kids lie still.
The kitchen clock is nodding in warm air.
They spread the Sunday paper on the table
And each draws up a comfortable chair.
He turns the pages to the crossword puzzle,
Nonplussed they see a single large black square.

The radio is playing dated music
With lilac tune and metronomic beat.
She smiles and says, 'Remember that one, darling?
The way we used to foxtrot was a treat.'
But they resist the momentary temptation
To resurrect slim dancers on glib feet.

In bed his tall enthusiastic member
Receives warm welcome, and a moist one too.
She whispers, 'Do you love me? More than ever?'
And, panting, he replies, 'Of course I do.'
Then as she sighs and settles close for slumber
He thinks with mild surprise that it is true.

VERNON SCANNELL

Newly-married couples love each other a great deal. But
there may be something superficial in this love, which has
to do with the excitement of discovery. Love is even deeper
between people who have been married for a long time,
who have lived through difficulties together and who know
that the other will be faithful until death. They know that
nothing can break their union.

JEAN VANIER

Bazin was a tall man, running to fat; soft-spoken, with a
delicate gentle face . . . We asked him how he managed in

169

La Fere. 'I am married,' he said, 'and I have my pretty children. But frankly, it is no life at all . . .'

We sat in front of the door, talking softly to Bazin . . . Madam Bazin came out after a while; she was tired with her day's work, I suppose, and she nestled up to her husband and laid her head upon his breast. He had his arm about her and kept gently patting her on the shoulder. I think Bazin was right, and he was really married. Of how few people can the same be said!

Little did the Bazins know how much they served us. We were charged for candles, for food and drink, and for the beds we slept in. But there was nothing in the bill for the husband's pleasant talk; nor for the pretty spectacle of their married life.

ROBERT LOUIS STEVENSON, *An Inland Voyage*

Now that the whirl of congratulations must be ceasing, here are mine, the latest but not the least warm of them all. You are going to marry one of the finest men in all the world, with a great store of sterling gifts of both head and heart, and with a life before him of the highest interest, importance and power. Such a man is a companion that any woman might envy you. I daresay you know this without my telling you. On the other part, I will not add myself to those impertinents who – as I understand you to report – wish you 'to improve'. I very respectfully wish nothing of the sort. Few qualities are better worth leaving as they are than vivacity, wit, freshness of mind, gaiety and pluck. Pray keep them all. Don't improve by an atom.

Circumstances may have a lesson or two to teach you, but 'tis only the dull who don't learn, and I have no fear but that such a pair have happy years in front of them.

You ask for my blessing and you have it. Be sure that I

wish you as unclouded a life as can be the lot of woman, and I hope you will always let me count myself your friend.

JOHN MORLEY TO MARGOT TENNANT (LATER ASQUITH),

7 MARCH 1894

A whole heart depends on both wisdom and the hopes forged out of that wisdom. I remember driving to my new home for the first time ... I had only recently passed my driving test, at the age of thirty-three, and found it odd that it was more difficult to get a driver's license than a marriage license. (Wouldn't it make sense to *earn* a marriage license? The multiple-choice and practical tests for a marriage license present intriguing possibilities. Can you imagine what the equivalent of parallel parking would be?) I was an especially cautious driver, as first-year drivers often are. I remember carefully adjusting the rearview mirror before I started out onto the highway so that I could make sure I knew what was behind me as well as in front of me.

In the bright sun of the late afternoon the gesture made sense on many levels. It certainly reminded me of my married life. I knew that by keeping my eyes on where I was going, as well as by not losing sight of where I had been, I could be safely on my way.

REGINA BARRECA, *PERFECT HUSBANDS (AND OTHER FAIRY TALES)*

It is only in romantic fiction that a man can work strenuously to the limit of his power and come home to be sweet, sunny and entertaining ...

And now, indeed, the Traffords were coming to the most difficult and fatal phase in marriage. They had had that taste of defiant adventure which is the crown of a spirited love affair, they had known the sweetness of a maiden

171

passion for a maid, and they had felt all those rich and solemn emotions, those splendid fears and terrible hopes that weave themselves about the great partnership in parentage. And now, so far as sex was concerned, there might be much joy and delight still, but no more wonder, no fresh discoveries of incredible new worlds and unsuspected stars. Love, which had been a new garden, an unknown land, a sunlit sea to launch upon, was now a rich treasure-house of memories. And memories, although they afford a perpetually increasing enrichment to emotion, are not sufficient in themselves for the daily needs of life.

For this, indeed, is the truth of passionate love, that it works out its purpose and comes to an end. A day arrives in every marriage when the lovers must face each other, disillusioned, stripped of the last shred of excitement – undisguisedly themselves.

H. G. WELLS, *MARRIAGE*

Within the couple relationship, the dissolving of barriers, the intimacy and the longing for closeness bring their own problems. Beginnings of relationships often seem so easy. There is usually terrific excitement, fluttery feelings, eagerness for sexual contact, lots of things to talk about with one another, desire to please the other by the way we dress, cook a meal, display attentiveness, etc. These beginnings of 'getting involved' seem almost effortless. For some couples, as time goes by, the sexual relationship and the channels of emotional understanding and communication get stronger and better. For many couples the love between two people grows and the connection deepens. For all couples there is some degree of friction and struggle. Disappointment and flare-ups happen as quickly as a flash of lightning, often for no apparent reason. Mood changes are affected dramatically and instantaneously. People un-wittingly have impulses to control or direct their partner. Partners withdraw from one another emotionally and physically, only to return again to closeness. Some people feel that, as time passes, they have less to talk about with their partner than in the early years or that their sexual interest has diminished.

From all the nuances and complications of couple relationships one central question stands out: if people so obviously need and search for contact and emotional intimacy, why is it that achieving this intimacy is at times so difficult or, to be more to the point, why is it that once we achieve a certain level of intimacy it is so difficult to sustain?

LUISE EICHENBAUM & SUSIE ORBACH, *WHAT DO WOMEN WANT?*

So few women have been as happy as I have been every hour since I married – so few have had such a wonderful sky of love for their common atmosphere, that perhaps it will seem strange when I write down that the sadness of Death and Parting is greatly lessened to me by the fact of my consciousness of the eternal, indivisible oneness of Alfred and me. I feel as long as he is down here I must be here silently, secretly sitting beside him as I do every evening now, however much my soul is the other side, and that if Alfred were to die, we would be as we were on earth, love as we did this year, only fuller, quicker, deeper than ever, with a purer passion and a wiser worship. Only in the meantime, whilst my body is hid from him and my eyes cannot see him, let my trivial toys be his till the morning comes when nothing will matter because all is spirit.

LAURA LYTTLETON, FROM HER WILL, QUOTED IN *THE AUTOBIOGRAPHY OF MARGOT ASQUITH*

Woke early to a glorious morning. The caterer and her minions were soon setting the bar up on a corner of the lawn, putting the little round tables and gilt chairs under the trees, and decorating the lunch table under the awning even better than I could have done it myself. And although the sun clouded over, it remained beautifully dry and warm so that people lolled on the grass just as we had dreamed. A real *fete-champetre*, as Ruth Adam called it. Only two things embarrassed me: the lavishness of the presents we had never expected and the collapse of Harold's deck chair under him. I learned later that a *Sunday Express* photographer, trying to take pictures through the hedge, had been beaten off by the combined efforts of our neighbour Dick Moore, and Ted's friend, Tony Boram, while Sonya burst into tears with fury, nearly beating him with her fists. Harold joined in the fun in a relaxed way, making suitable cracks as he planted the commemoration tree, while our Tory friends were enchanted with Mary Wilson. An idyllic party in which I was actually able to join because I wasn't in the kitchen rustling up food. At 6 p.m., as the last guests were saying they ought to go, the first raindrops fell.

BARBARA CASTLE ON HER AND TED'S SILVER WEDDING,
26 JULY 1969

(The Harold whose deck chair collapsed is Harold, later Lord, Wilson, Labour Prime Minister 1964–6, 1966–70, 1974–6; Mary is his wife.)

Perhaps, she thought, true lovers keep on finding each other all through their lives.

H. G. WELLS, *MARRIAGE*

Women love too much; they allow love to over-ride everything else. Men don't. Or, rather, men see to it that the

people who love them should submit themselves. I love
you too much. You are much more important to me than
anything else. That is the long and short of the matter. But,
darling, I am not a good person for you to be married to –
said she, avoiding the word wife. When people like you
and me marry – *positive* people, when men and women
ought to be positive and negative respectively, complementary elements – life resolves itself into a compromise
which is truly satisfactory to neither. But I love you; I can
never never never cure myself of loving you; so what is to
be done? And you love foreign politics. And I love
literature, and peace, and a secluded life. Oh my dear, my
infinitely dear Hadji, you never ought to have married me;
and I feel my inadequacy most bitterly. What good am I to
you? None. What with one thing and another.

But at least I do love you, incurably, ineradicably, and
most oddly. That remains, fixed. Immutable.

VITA SACKVILLE-WEST TO HAROLD NICOLSON,
13 DECEMBER 1928

You are dearer to me than anybody ever has been or ever
could be . . . Every time I get you to myself you become
dearer to me. I do not think one could conceive of a love
more exclusive, more tender, or more pure than that I have
for you. It is absolutely divorced from physical love – sex –
now. I feel it is immortal, I am superstitious about it, I feel
it is a thing which happens seldom. I suppose that everybody who falls in love feels this about their love, and that
for them it is merely a platitude. But then when one falls in
love it is all mixed up with physical desire, which is the
most misleading of all human emotions, and most readily
and convincingly wears the appearance of the real thing.
This does not enter at all into my love for you. I simply feel
that you are me and I am you – what you meant by saying

that you 'became the lonely me' when we parted.

Darling, there are not many people who would write such a love letter after nearly sixteen years of marriage, yet who would be saying therein only one-fiftieth of what they were feeling as they wrote it. But you know not only that it is true, every word, but that it represents only a pale version of the real truth – I could not exaggerate, however much I tried – I don't try. I try sometimes to tell you the truth and then I find that I have no words at my command which could possibly convey it to you.

VITA SACKVILLE-WEST TO HAROLD NICOLSON, 25 JUNE 1929

Harold Nicolson's and Vita Sackville-West's son comments on his parents' letters:

Reiterated expressions of mutual love between husband and wife are said to be unnecessary if it is genuine and strongly rooted, but Vita and Harold felt the need to reassure each other constantly of what both profoundly believed, so amazed were they that the marriage had survived its first traumatic ten years to become for both of them a life-enhancing success in the remaining forty.

NIGEL NICOLSON

My latest and my final love was a Russian who had no connections with the ballet . . . She was reading history at the Sorbonne and had finally settled in Paris after the long trek from Kiev via Constantinople, Berlin and Brussels. The minute I set eyes on her I knew I was going to marry her, and wrote so to my best friend, although I was still engaged to the Monte Carlo girl. We went to dances, opera and ballet together, and in spite of our having few tastes, though many ideas, in common I knew it would work. When I finally decided to propose I took her to the Louvre

– she says it was to test her reaction to my favourite paintings; it may have been – then to lunch at Rumplemayers and when I had summoned up enough courage, into the Tuileries Gardens. As soon as I proposed she asked my advice and I told her she had better accept. We were both twenty-one . . .

I have never for a moment regretted that afternoon in the Tuileries. My wife has been a marvel of patience, but to me her supreme virtue is that she has never bored me. We have given one another perfect freedom which neither has abused. My marriage has been the most fortunate, and also the most intelligent thing I have ever done.

ARNOLD HASKELL, *IN HIS TRUE CENTRE*

We have been married for more than thirty-two years: we are both nearly sixty: . . . I am, in many ways, an impossible man to live with: and she has one or two characteristics which, when I am at my most intolerant, I find intensely and recurrently irritating. But – though 'but' is not at all the right word – we know consciously on our honeymoons, what we have known less consciously every minute of our lives since a month before our wedding, that our marriage has been essentially – it is a very large claim, and you must note the word 'essentially' – perfect: and that a marriage which is perfect, even if only essentially, would be sufficient justification, in the absence of all other justifications, for the sum of things. 'Blessed art thou, O Lord, who makest the bridegroom to rejoice with the bride.'

I mean by a honeymoon a time of some length when we are always together. From the middle twenties till about 1937 we were constantly having honeymoons . . . The world, at such times, was no longer with us: we were with one another in the world. There have been many other times, of course, every week since we were married, when our lives have had the same sort of feel: Friday evenings at Brimpton, motoring to the Cotswolds, and those lunches or dinners, by ourselves, at a London restaurant, when affairs have dropped momentarily away from us and, both a little tight, we have been wholly together. But these are not real honeymoons; they are too short, too quickly over; intimations of a honeymoon, you might say, rather than the thing itself . . .

Of all our New York honeymoons, this last one – perhaps because every year now one learns a little better how to live – has been the best . . . the fever and strain were enclosed, as perhaps never before, in the peace of our togetherness.

When I attempt to particularise, I find myself thinking, very oddly, first about food. Or perhaps it isn't odd. Love-feasts are to be found, after all, in the ritual of more than one religion: and everyone understands that the breaking of bread is a sacrament, if at least two are present. Why this is so I cannot tell. Perhaps we feel very obscurely that at a common meal the unity of men with one another, and of humanity with earth, is realised.

Our love-feasts were the meals Ruth prepared in our diminutive kitchen, and that we ate at a little glass-topped table, sitting side by side on a sofa: breakfast in particular, quiet and slow, with its sense of a recurrent expectancy and a recurrent fulfilment. Even the happiest meals with others were not love-feasts. We had to be alone.

VICTOR GOLLANCZ, *MY DEAR TIMOTHY: AN AUTOBIOGRAPHICAL LETTER TO HIS GRANDSON*

Tevye:	Golde, I'm asking you a question – Do you love me?
Golde:	You're a fool.
Tevye:	I know – But do you love me?
Golde:	Do I love you?

For twenty-five years I've washed your clothes,
Cooked your meals, cleaned your house,
Given you children, milked the cow,
After twenty-five years, why talk about
Love right now?

Tevye: Golde, the first time I met you
Was on our wedding day.
I was scared.

Golde: I was shy.

Tevye: I was nervous.

Golde: So was I.

Tevye: But my father and my mother
Said we'd learn to love each other.
And now I'm asking, Golde,
Do you love me?

Golde: I'm your wife.

Tevye: I know – But do you love me?

Golde: Do I love him?
For twenty-five years I've lived with him
Fought with him, starved with him
Twenty-five years my bed is his.
If that's not love, what is?

Tevye: Then you love me?

Golde: I suppose I do.

Tevye: And I suppose I love you, too.

Tevye and Golde: It doesn't change a thing,
But even so,
After twenty-five years,
It's nice to know.

JOSEPH STEIN, *FIDDLER ON THE ROOF*

The Murphys from Manchester who married in 1947:

They come from a generation who stuck at marriage, for whom divorce was rarely an option. Some marriages, they acknowledge, were more successful than others, but they don't see their longstanding happiness as a particularly unusual achievement and it saddens them that it is viewed as such today.

'Now it's all about sex,' says Margaretha. 'Relationships don't seem as sincere and people run away from responsibility.' Her husband puts the rising divorce rate down to the pressure of modern life. 'It was far simpler in our times. We'd suffered through the war and people wanted to make the best of things. Materially we had nothing, but we didn't expect anything either. There were no leisure facilities so we had to make our own leisure and that brought families together.'

They talk easily to each other and have never had secrets. 'When we've had worries about the children we've always talked them through,' says Margaretha. 'We've done everything together from the day we've first met, and I'm quite sure that's why we've had such a wonderful marriage. I've never had any trouble from him, he's never wanted to play cards or go down the pub, we've always preferred to be at home reading or watching the telly together.'

There have been no troughs of real unhappiness in this marriage, only harmony and a huge attachment for each other. Margaretha feels the love and appreciation she has for her husband grows deeper by the day, and most days she tells him so. Life alone is an unbearable prospect but they see their interdependence as a sign of strength, rather than a weakness. Margaretha frequently says to her husband: 'If anything happens to you, you have to take me with you, or else I'll kill you.' His teasing reply is: 'If I'm dead already how can you kill me?'

It is a marriage free of resentment, blame and power struggles. 'On the very rare occasions that we row we never go to bed without having made up. I don't believe in sleeping on it,' says John. When he declares that he's never lifted a hand to his wife, you have to remember that the Murphys grew up at a time when it was considered acceptable for a man to use force to keep women in place.

Margaretha puts the success of her children's marriages down to the fact that they have parents who love each other. 'Loving and cuddling children counts for everything, because if you don't receive love you don't know how to give it.'

MARINA CANTACUZINO IN THE *OBSERVER REVIEW*,
19 JANUARY 1977

Lying apart now, each in a separate bed,
He with a book, keeping the light on late,
She like a girl dreaming of childhood,
All men elsewhere – it is as if they wait
Some new event: the book he holds unread,
Her eyes fixed on the shadows overhead.

Tossed up like flotsam from a former passion,
How cool they lie. They hardly ever touch,
Of if they do it is like a confession
Of having little feeling – or too much.
Chastity faces them, a destination
For which their whole lives were a preparation.

Strangely apart, yet strangely together,
Silence between them like a thread to hold
And not wind in. And time itself's a feather
Touching them gently. Do they know they're old,

Weddings

These two who are my father and my mother
Whose fire, from which I came, has now grown cold?

Elizabeth Jennings

In the *Daily Mail* of 8 March 1987, Paul Johnson, writer and critic, on his fortieth wedding anniversary wrote of 'The Secrets of Marriage':

> What must be faced is that no marriage is easy. Very few people are naturally 'good' at marriage. Most marriages spring from love, but they have to be consolidated by skill, persistence, industry. Young people – middle-aged people for that matter – have to learn to work at it. It is an art, a profession, a job. You might call it the most difficult unpaid job in the world.
>
> And I'm sorry to have to say it, the woman has to do most of the work. Biology has cast the man in the role of villain and the woman as heroine. As that wise and much tried woman Queen Marie of Romania puts it: 'A woman's virtue must indeed be great, since it often has to suffice for two' . . .
>
> A saving grace in marriage, I think, is to identify a salient fault and work at it. Bad temper kills a lot of marriages and I know I suffer from it . . .
>
> My one great virtue is jokes. Humour is a vital element in marriage and it is odd that the Marriage Service says nothing about it . . .
>
> I would strongly advise a woman never to dream of marrying a man unless she is certain he can make her smile, laughs at her wit (most women are witty) and laughs at himself. Most polls show women rate 'sense of humour' at or near the top of the qualities they look for in a man – quite rightly. Humour becomes more important in marriage as it endures, because it is garnished by old

shared jokes and remembered laughter.

Both of us are good at forgiveness. All marriages are composed of light and shade and punctuated by crimes and misdemeanours. Feelings of resentment at them must not be bottled up but allowed to express themselves colourfully – and then the episode kissed away and, if possible, forgotten.

A marriage in which resentment is harboured and revenge plotted is doomed. As Francis Bacon says, 'It is a prince's part to pardon.' A union in which forgiveness is humbly sought and freely granted is no ordinary one but a marriage between a prince and princess.

Another salient virtue in marriage is loyalty. This is not to be confused with fidelity. Absolute fidelity in marriage, though always desirable, is rarely to be expected these days.

But its occasional absence can be accommodated, granted forgiveness and the fundamental loyalty which makes husbands and wives see each other as (to quote Sherlock Holmes on Dr Watson) 'the one fixed point in a changing world'.

A married couple may argue, even fight, against each other. But they must always close ranks against a common enemy.

How one couple adapted their relationship to suit each other:

Charles and Elizabeth Handy are enjoying their second marriage or is it their third? They cannot quite decide. They have not, as Taylor and Burton did, split up and come together again. Instead they have spotted the tensions in their 34-year-old union and renegotiated.

'Did you rebel as a teenager?' they ask, as one, over lunch. 'If you didn't, you might in middle age and then run out on your marriage. We have many friends who have split.

The husband says "now you've done your bit with the kids, I don't know your friends . . . and there's this nice woman at work."'

Charles Handy is a man who analyses situations . . . He wrote *The Age of Unreason* (1989) in which he considered marriage. An A-A marriage, for example, was one between two gregarious equals, characterised by muddle and discussion. A B-B marriage was between two ambitious individuals, involving intense competition. A B-D marriage consisted of an achiever and a supporter – classic but likely to hit trouble.

His own marriage, he realised, had been classic B-D: he had earned the money, while Elizabeth cared for the family. Judderingly, they had shifted to an A-A. Then, two-and-a-half years ago, they renegotiated again and now have, virtually, a B-B set-up – 'but we're not competitive'.

They call theirs a portfolio marriage: instead of changing partners, they have adjusted their relationship. On the same principle, they have never moved house, just adapted the old one. 'You can change your home, your marriage, your life,' is their message.

Exhaustive and detailed planning is a feature of their current two-career set-up. Elizabeth is a photographer and so, during the light summer months, her work takes precedence. 'I've had to say no to things I'd like to do,' says Charles, 'because they are in her time.'

On October 1, it became Charles's turn to dictate where they are and what they do. 'The rule, and the purpose, is that we debate exceptions,' he explains.

Such careful planning is needed because, when they switched to the equal partners arrangement, they discovered they wanted to be together all the time . . .

'We decided that if she worked with me, but not for me – and if we could carve out time and space for each other –

then it would be like marrying the person you work with. Like marrying a second time,' he says . . . then for the third phase in their marriage, Elizabeth decided she wanted her own career. Again, they discussed their relationship and developed the system of diary priority . . .

'If you can grow together, you are more tolerant and complementary to each other,' he says.

'Our children are very worried about us,' adds Elizabeth. 'We are more in love than we ever were' . . . The Handys have found they need each other – and it is a recipe for happiness that other couples could try.

CASSANDRA JARDINE IN THE *Daily Telegraph*,
15 NOVEMBER 1996

The ring so worn as you behold,
So thin, so pale, is yet of gold:
The passion such it was to prove;
Worn with life's care, love yet was love.

GEORGE CRABBE, 'A MARRIAGE RING'

Advice to a Husband

The next thing to be attended to is, your demeanour towards a young wife. As to oldish ones, or widows, time and other things have, in most cases, blunted their feelings, and rendered harsh or stern demeanour in the husband a matter not of heart-breaking consequence. But with a young and inexperienced one the case is very different; and you should bear in mind that the first frown that she receives from you is a dagger to her heart. Nature has so ordered it, that men shall become less ardent in their passion after the wedding-day, and that women shall not. Their ardour increases rather than the contrary; and they are surprisingly quick-sighted and inquisitive on this score. When the child comes, it divides this ardour with the father; but until then, you have it all; and if you have a mind to be happy, repay it with all your soul. Let what may happen to put you out of humour with others, let nothing put you out of humour with her. Let your words and looks and manners be just what they were before you called her wife.

But now, and throughout your life, show your affection for her, and your admiration of her, not in nonsensical compliment; not in picking up her handkerchief or her glove, or in carrying her fan or parasol; not, if you have the means, in hanging trinkets and baubles upon her; not in making yourself a fool by winking at, and seeming pleased at, her foibles, or follies, or faults; but show them by acts of real goodness towards her; prove by unequivocal deeds the high value that you set on her health and life and peace of mind; let your praise of her go to the full extent of her deserts; but let it be consistent with truth and with sense, and such as to convince her of your sincerity. He who is the flatterer of his wife only prepares her ears for the hyperbolic stuff of others. The kindest appellation that her Christian name affords is the best you can use, especially before faces. An everlasting 'my dear' is but a sorry compensation for a want of that sort of love that makes the husband cheerfully toil by day, break his rest by night, endure all sorts of hardships, if the life or health of his wife demand it. Let your deeds, and not your words, carry to her heart a daily and hourly confirmation of the fact, that you value her health and life and happiness beyond all other things in the world; and let this be manifest to her, particularly at those times when life is always more or less in danger.

WILLIAM COBBETT, *ADVICE TO YOUNG MEN AND WOMEN*

A permanent address, regular sex, and home-cooked meals seemed to be enough for a number of men who were raised to hold on to traditional expectations (in fact, a number of them would have settled for home-cooked sex, permanent meals, and a regular address). These men were often the most keenly disappointed after marriage. They thought they understood what they were getting into, only to find that much more was demanded of them than they expected. They felt that marriage was a bargain they didn't bargain for, 'like signing up for two free books and then having to buy a hundred books a year for the next forty years,' as one older insurance salesman put it. 'I thought I'd hand her my paycheck – well, most of it anyway – and she'd hand me a couple of children, a clean house, and a couple of cozy bedtimes. Instead she wanted me to talk all night. It wasn't what I figured on, I'll tell you that.' This man is well over sixty, but the young men with whom I've spoken sound as if these last forty years haven't made much of an impact on their expectations, hopes, and fears for themselves as husbands.

. . . a man can expect to keep the same name, same job, same social status, same standard of living, and, often, the same dwelling after he marries. Traditional marriage ceremonies pronounce the couple 'man' and 'wife'. He is a man, presumably, even before the ceremony, otherwise she wouldn't be tempted to marry him; he *stays* a man, she *becomes* a wife. He will also expect, not surprisingly, to be able to keep his personality, habits, and customs. It is said that troubles arise after the wedding because a woman marries a man expecting him to change and is disappointed when he doesn't, and that a man marries expecting a woman not to change, and she does.

REGINA BARRECA, *PERFECT HUSBANDS (AND OTHER FAIRY TALES)*

When a man hath taken a new wife, he shall not go out to war, neither shall he be charged with any business: but he shall be free at home one year, and shall cheer up his wife which he hath taken.

DEUTERONOMY 24:5

There is no such thing as a perfect marriage. Marriage keeps us humble. The safest way to become humble about one's virtues is to get married.

WALTER TROBISCH, *I MARRIED YOU*

Her Face is to me much more beautiful than when I first saw it; there is no Decay in any Feature, which I cannot trace from the very Instant it was occasioned by some anxious Concern for my Welfare and Interests . . . Oh! she is an inestimable Jewel.

SIR RICHARD STEELE, 'MR BICKERSTAFF VISITS A FRIEND',
TATLER, NO. 95

Advice to a Wife

Above all else, the most important thing in my life is my husband. To have had a happy marriage is a very good thing.

IRIS MURDOCH, IN THE *DAILY MAIL*, 17 AUGUST 1996

Johnson told me, with an amiable fondness, a little pleasing circumstance relative to this work. Mrs Johnson, in whose judgement and taste he had great confidence, said to him, after a few numbers of *The Rambler* had come out, 'I thought very well of you before; but I did not imagine you could have written any thing equal to this.' Distant praise, from whatever quarter, is not so delightful as that of a wife whom a man loves and esteems. Her

188

approbation may be said to 'come home to his bosom;' and being so near, its effect is most sensible and permanent.

JAMES BOSWELL, THE LIFE OF SAMUEL JOHNSON

Advice given to Eleanor (Bunny) Roosevelt on her marriage to Theodore Roosevelt, Jr., by a friend:

> Don't be a yes-woman. Tell Ted frankly when you agree or disapprove . . . Never take him for granted. If you don't listen with sympathy and warmth whenever he tells you anything about himself, remember there are plenty of other women who will.

> A visiting wife describes her husband as a good one, and gives me as a definition, 'He doesn't get drunk *every* Saturday.'

THE REVEREND J. W. HORSLEY, 27 AUGUST 1886

Indeed, my dear young friend, you have highly obliged me by such a distinguishing mark of friendship and consideration as that of finding time, on the most important day of your life, to inform me with your own hand of your marriage: an event most interesting to me, who wish your happiness with the sincerest ardour. You tell me you expect from me, not a letter of formal congratulation, but of serious and friendly advice on the new situations and duties in which you are going to be engaged . . .

I know you have not been brought up in modish principles, and that you do not at present consider marriage as a title to unbounded liberty and perpetual dissipation, instead of a solemn engagement to subjection and obedience, to family cares and serious employments. You will probably, indeed, meet with people who will

189

endeavour to laugh you out of all such regards, and who will find something very ludicrous in the idea of authority in a husband. But, whatever your opinions may be on this head, it is certain that a man of Mr B.'s generosity would be much mortified and distressed to find himself obliged to exert his authority in restraining your pleasures, particularly on his first setting out with you on the journey of life.

HESTER CHAPONE TO A NEW-MARRIED LADY

In the early days of my marriage the formulas of feminism pestered me because I allowed my husband to support me. But since I had used my economic independence previously as a means to adventure, and the immediate adventure of my life was the entirely unforeseen one of adjusting to intimacy and conflict in marriage, I found it easy to still the accusing voice which pointed out that principles were at stake. Besides which, having found that most of my principles were generated out of perversity, it became necessary as I grew older either to cast rigid rules of conduct out altogether or to invent them as the situation arose or to remold new ones out of a more adult attitude. My feminism is a part of my ego and perhaps nothing more. I like myself – and I am a woman. Therefore, I naturally resent injustice on the basis of sex.

ANONYMOUS QUAKER

It is unlikely that young married women today would be as passive as these military wives:

Each in her separate house the young wives sit
  Alone from six to nine.
Though they be dear and beautiful and gay,

They never drink with friends or see a play,
   They never dance or dine.
Patient, the wives of Territorials sit and knit.

Straight from his work the model husband goes
   To distant dusty grounds.
Bathed in the ruddy setting of the sun,
He polishes a non-existent gun,
   Fires off imaginary rounds.
At home his wife droops like an autumn rose.

Virginia Graham

Fling wide the curtains! – that's a Surrey sunset!
   Low down the line sings the Addiscombe train,
Leaded are the windows lozenging the crimson,
   Drained dark the pines in resin-scented rain.
Portable Lieutenant! they carry you to China
   And me to a lonely shopping in a brilliant arcade:
Firm hand, fond hand, switch the giddy engine!
   So for us a last time is bright light made

John Betjeman

From a mother to a daughter suspicious of her husband:

> You have no *proof* that he is guilty, but your surmizes, or,
> perhaps, the busy *whisperings* of officious *make-debates*.
> In this case, take care, my Betsey, that you don't by
> the violence of your passions, precipitate him on the
> course you dread, and that you alienate not, by unjust
> suspicion, his affections from you; for then perhaps
> he will be ready *indeed* to place them somewhere
> else, whence you may not so easily draw him off; for
> he will, may be, think, as to *you* (if he be devoid of
> *superior* considerations), that he may as well *deserve* your

suspicions, as be teased with them *without* deserving them.

SAMUEL RICHARDSON, *LETTERS WRITTEN TO AND FOR
PARTICULAR FRIENDS, DIRECTING THE REQUISITE STYLE AND
FORMS TO BE OBSERVED IN WRITING FAMILIAR LETTERS*

If it's tiresome to have a jealous husband, it must be humiliating to have one who is not.

MARGOT ASQUITH

Breakdown and Divorce

It wasn't, I told myself, as if I was really giving in. Like the heroine in one of my favourite plays, I vowed that I wasn't going to 'by degrees dwindle into a wife.' I bought my own wedding ring and bargained it down to a reasonable price; it was going to be a modern marriage. He didn't own me, so why should he be made to put a piece of gold on my finger? The ring I bought did not even look like an ordinary wedding band; I told myself that I was subverting the rituals of matrimony even as I came under their spell.

The trouble was, I didn't see the mechanics of this trick I played on myself: For all my protestations, I still wore a ring on the third finger of my left hand. And I liked the feeling. Amazing transformations occurred, all in my own mind, but they occurred nonetheless. I reverted to the ideas I'd been taught as a child. It took no time at all for me to put away the independence I'd flaunted for ten years. With this wedding ring, I suddenly felt unreasonably safe in the subway as if no lunatic would bother me now. With this ring, I felt secure in the classroom, believing my students would whisper in relief, 'See? You can be a feminist and still get a man.' With this ring, I felt confident at my high school reunion: I *was* attractive, and a committed man lived under my roof. It was as if I were surrounded by a kind of marriage-magic that could ward off all unhappiness.

But it was a sham: It was not a magical ring or a magical marriage. What I thought offered safety instead offered captivity. By pretending not to be part of a 'real marriage,' we could not support the weight of the real concerns of our life together. We buckled under the strain, and the relationship ended after six years.

REGINA BARRECA, *PERFECT HUSBANDS (AND OTHER FAIRY TALES)*

Reader, a marriage that is rapidly put together can rapidly unravel: like a hand-knitted jumper, which if you snip just one strand and pull, and go on pulling, comes to nothing at all. Just a pile of wrinkled junk. Or put it another way: you think you're living in a palace but actually it's just a house of cards. Disturb one card and the whole lot falls and flattens and is nothing.

FAY WELDON, *THE HEARTS AND LIVES OF MEN*

Novelist Margaret Drabble strikes a warning note in her novel, *The Waterfall*:

It is a curious business, marriage. Nobody seems to pay enough attention to its immense significance. Nobody seemed to think that in approaching the altar, garbed in white, I was walking toward unknown disaster of unforeseeable proportions: and so I tried to emulate – I emulated successfully – the world's fine, confident unconcern. Such an emulation had paid off so well on so many other alarming occasions (anaesthesia, for instance, or diving off the top diving board, both events which, I was assured, despite a natural reluctant fear, would not harm me) that I was prepared to take the world's calm view of marriage too, distrusting and ignoring the forebodings that even then possessed me: in such a mood, assured that it is a normal event or a commonplace sacrifice, one might well lay one's head upon the block or jump from a high window.

MARGARET DRABBLE, THE WATERFALL

Some think any wives good enough, who have but goods enough – But take heed, for sometimes the bag and baggage go together. Marriages are styled matches – yet amongst those many that are married, how few are there matched. Husbands and wives are like locks and keys, that rather break than open, except the wards be answerable.

THE REVEREND JOHN THOMLINSON

As a result of my experience, and of much experience in the courts and elsewhere of the facts of other people's marriages, I have changed my views concerning remarriage after divorce. I continue to think of marriage as sacramental in character, and, in a life lived responsibly, it ought to be for life, and to impose a life-long obligation of mutual fidelity. But the fact is that marriages do break down, sometimes from the fault of one only of the parties, sometimes of both, occasionally as the result of circumstances outside the control of either. In such cases I believe that to impose an obligation of life-long celibacy on either or both of the parties terminable only on what has become the irrelevant duration of the other's life is in the interest neither of public or private morality, nor, indeed, of religious observance. I say this humbly, realizing as I do how difficult this view is to reconcile with the explicit teaching of the gospels and of the largest denomination in the Christian Church. None the less I have to say on this subject: 'I can no other.' I ought to add one footnote. I do not agree with those churchmen who allege, without I believe the smallest evidence, that all marital breakdowns are due to faults on both sides. Of course, none of us being perfect, no one of us is perfection in any human relationship either within the family or outside it. But what I write is based on a more than averagely wide experience of other people's marital affairs, and not only upon my own. Moreover I have heard judges of experience in family law much wider than mine, including one President of the Family Division, give voice to the same opinion. Before 1969, the secular law concerning divorce was fundamentally based on fault, and the courts, and therefore the profession, had to delve more deeply into the conduct of the parties than is now desirable or permissible. While I accept that in all human relationships no one is ever without fault, I personally seldom found the smallest difficulty, whether professionally or advising friends, given the requisite information, in deciding which of the two parties, or whether both of them, was or were responsible for the actual breakdown of a marriage, and this I believe to be the considered view of most of those who have professional experience on the subject. When I think of what my life would have been like in the past forty-five years without my marriage to Mary and without, eight years after Mary's death, marriage to my present wife, I tremble to think what would have become of me.

LORD HAILSHAM, *A SPARROW'S FLIGHT: MEMOIRS*

The real crux of any divorce law is about money and property, or about children, or both. It was true when I first practised at the Bar from 1932 onwards. It was true in 1979 at the commencement of my second term. It is true today. The use of the civil law to hold together parties who wish to live separately is almost always misguided. What ought to be explained to parties who contemplate divorce is that, although a marriage may or may not be brought to an end, the consequences of divorce are long-lived and may be permanent.

. . . The real trouble about the proliferation of divorces is partly that parties who enter into a marriage only too often do so without a real intention to make it permanent, and too often allow a temporary quarrel or a casual and perhaps almost venial act of infidelity to be made the occasion of a permanent separation.

. . . The churches had been much too ready to say that in every case both parties were to blame. Since no one is perfect, this is quite possibly true. But I have heard it said – I think it was by Lord Simon of Glaisdale – and it is certainly my own experience, that although obviously in the course of matrimonial estrangement both parties had from time to time committed faults it was seldom difficult to identify the party really responsible for the final break-down. The relevance of this fact to the various questions to be argued after dissolution varies from the trivial to the decisive . . .

The difficulties of ignoring the previous conduct of the parties during marriage were accentuated by the total impossibility of ignoring the behaviour of the parties, good or bad, after divorce. This was all the more unjust because the types of such conduct differed from the exemplarily good to the appallingly bad . . . Once bitterness and antagonism have set in there is practically no length to which ex-partners will not go to assuage their own unhappiness or advance their interests, real or supposed, at the expense of the other party . . . Baseless accusations proliferate, and each class of evil compounds the effects of the others.

LORD HAILSHAM, *A SPARROW'S FLIGHT: MEMOIRS*

The expectations we have of the institution of marriage in Western society in the latter half of the twentieth century are truly remarkable. The three cardinal features of the Judaeo-Christian vision of marriage – its indissolubility, its emphasis on child-bearing and fidelity – still exercise a powerful appeal. Within marriage we are encouraged to find intimacy, companionship and dependence. But the newer values of what has been termed the human potential movement which began to emerge during the 1950s and 1960s suggest that within marriage the partners are also engaged in a search to find themselves and each other; both searches are lifelong and neither is guaranteed to progress in such a way as to ensure the survival of the marriage itself. Where once marriage was seen through prosaic eyes as a public contract legitimising sexual union, embodying a permanent social relationship and prescribing certain obligations regarding family, parenthood and a place of residence, now it is viewed through more rosy spectacles and the stated goals include personal growth, sexual fulfilment and mutual emotional satisfaction.

ANTHONY CLARE, *LOVELAW*

This emphasis on the importance of fidelity persists despite the increase in life expectation following improvements in public health which now means that many couples face an undissolved marital relationship spanning forty or fifty years, compared with the fifteen or twenty years experienced by their not so remote ancestors. Despite this increase in the expected duration of marriage, there is still a persistent tendency to view the marriage that ends in divorce as a failure.

ANTHONY CLARE, *LOVELAW*

The proportion of the eligible population that marries is . . . as high as it has ever been while the number of remarriages has paralelled that of divorce.

What appears to be happening is that we are moving towards a pattern of two or more marriages in a lifetime. But remarriages are no more likely to be enduring. Marriages involving spouses who have been married before are about twice as likely to end in divorce as those that involve partners who have had no previous marital partners. Indeed, current remarriage rates in Britain are such that about one in three of all marriages are a second or subsequent one for at least one of the spouses.

Wherever we look marriage appears vulnerable. Yet the expectation that marriage will prove indissoluble remains an entrenched one in the minds of most people embarking on married life.

ANTHONY CLARE, *LOVELAW*

It is doubtful . . . that a cheapening of the ideal of marriage has either contributed to or been produced by the provision of easier forms of divorce. Everywhere one looks, one encounters highly idealised and highly demanding expectations of what marriage as an institution can provide. It is precisely because marriage is so revered that it breaks down so frequently.

ANTHONY CLARE, *LOVELAW*

Simon Jenkins writes in *The Times*, 15 June 1996, of Lord Mackay's Family Law Bill:

Its intention is not to make divorce easier or harder. It is to make this final trauma of a failed marriage less acrimonious, less expensive and less damaging to children. Lawyers would have a smaller role to play and mediators (not conciliators) a larger one. After all, the Bill seeks to remove the concept of marital fault from the law of divorce, 'to get the lawyer out of the marriage bed' . . . The essence of this reform . . . is that the state's task is to order relations between private citizens, not pass judgement on those relations.

A divorce is not a blessing granted by a stern state only to those who can push a pea down a Family Division corridor in the Law Courts. It is a human and civil right. The breakdown of a marriage has consequences for property and children, which the law must regulate. Where the law is breached, punishment is appropriate. But it is not the job of the law to punish by blame, acrimony and public humiliation those who break their marriage vows, for reasons that are of no public concern.

Mira Kirshenbaum, the American psychotherapist and author of *Too Good to Leave, Too Bad to Stay*, wrote in the *Independent* magazine in February 1997 of the need to diagnose a relationship that is breaking down. Two of the thirty-six diagnostic questions and their possible responses are:

> *If one of you did something to profoundly hurt the other – such as have an affair – has the pain and damage diminished over time?* A 'no' means *leave*. When our research began we were curious about whether affairs were generally fatal to relationships. But betrayal is a weird disease: it's the side-effects that will kill you . . . it's not betrayal but damaged trust that's fatal. This question gets at the fact that it's not damage but failure to heal that points to a mortal wound. The healing may happen very slowly like a clock that seems not to move because you're staring at it. Still, if you notice that more time means less pain, there's hope for you. But if, like a broken clock, the hurt is always at the same level, damage has been done to your ability to trust or forgive that makes this relationship too bad to stay in.

Do you feel it's possible for the two of you to have fun together? This question is actually about intimacy. People complain all the time about wishing they were closer to their partners or about needing distance from their partners. But what is it about intimacy that people cherish most? It's not poking a torch into the darkest corners of the heart. It's laughing together. It's a bit of play that no one else sees. You may not be what anyone else thinks of as fun people, and you may not be having a lot of fun these days, but if your answer is no and you no longer think that fun is possible between you, then leaving will be your best choice. Fun is the glue of love, and when it's gone love comes unglued.

Vanessa Berridge, 'When a Marriage Collapses' in *Sainsbury's Magazine*, March 1997.

Marriage is a very personal contract between two people which needs constant renegotiation. Fewer areas than in the past can be taken for granted: women expect to have careers rather than staying at home, looking after their children and absorbing their husbands' professional pressures . . .

A significant change, and one that is welcomed by psychotherapist, author and former Relate spokesperson Zelda West-Meads, is the disappearance of the social stigma of divorce. 'It is accepted that there are many different types of family and, although most people believe it is better for children to be brought up in a two-parent family, it needs to be a loving family. If the couple is constantly at war, that can be as destructive as separation and divorce – sometimes more so.

'Divorce is always heartbreaking. Very often you get one person who is desperately trying to hold on to the marriage and the other saying "I want out".'

The Family Act introduced the concept of a 'No-Fault' divorce. Despite outcry from some quarters that it would make divorce easier, it has been largely welcomed by marriage support organizations ... 'The Family Act,' says Zelda West-Meads, 'should take the sting out of divorce. Instead of trying to prove unreasonable behaviour to get a divorce in under two years, couples should be able to put the needs of their children and their own needs to the fore. However well intentioned you are in the beginning, if you have to attribute blame, you are likely to become more entrenched in disliking your partner and fight back to the detriment of all.'

Rob Heyland writes on the midlife crisis in *YOU* magazine, 19 January 1997:

Where has it all gone wrong? When I was young marriage was right there with mum, God and the monarchy: you could depend on it. In our small town of 15,000 there was one divorce, and the reverberations could still be felt down at the Bridge Stores months later ... Divorce – it meant defeat, disgrace and disgust. It was the devil.

[The author and his wife were snowed in at New Year with two friends – one a woman, one a man – each of whom had just separated from their partners.] I was startled by so many things – how love turns to hate; by the fact that people are so surprised when it happens to them; by the awful thrill of love and passion in a new relationship; by the terrible pain of guilt and betrayal, as much to do with letting down one's children as one's partner; by the fearful distance that can quickly grow between people who were so close and who shared so much; by the fact that the grass actually is greener when you see how terribly joyless and sexless and lacking in generosity so many marriages appear to be; by the fact that even those happily married have strong desires to sleep with other people and probably would if they could get away with it; by how many marriages are ending or are held together with string for the sake of the children; and most of all, by a creeping sensation that it could happen to me.

I am a midlifer. For all the joy I get from my wife and my children, I have the nagging worry that, as the children are growing up and away, my central relationship is being thrown into stark relief. I know the temptations of adventure, new love, new passion, new energy. I live with battles over homework, paying the mortgage, weight gain and sagging skin, with exhaustion and boredom. I accept the duty and the responsibility but I also feel its weight. I worry that the best of my life is over and that I'm now consigned to dribbling inconsequentially down the hill to incoherence, impotence and death.

Being Apart

I am lying here worn out, among the remotest tribes and regions . . . And . . . you, my wife . . . occupy more than your equal share in my heart. My voice names you only; no night, no day comes to me without you . . . your name is ever on my wandering lips.

OVID

While the leaves of the bamboo rustle
On a cold and frosty night,
The seven layers of clobber I wear
Are not so warm, not so warm
As the body of my wife.

TRANS. FROM THE JAPANESE GEOFFREY BOWNAS AND
ANTHONY THWAITE

My only sweetheart,

The great desire I have to see thee keeps alive thine image in me, and the extraordinary love which I receive from thee makes me discover mine with as much zeal as my poor understanding will afford, for I am sure I do outlove you, and will be a precedent for all mankind if ever I have to show how a husband ought to love as good a wife. Be happy in all thou thinkest of me, if any deserts in me can make thee so, for be assured that I will never change. God bless the child and make him a Saint George, and let not your prayers be wanting for your true friend and loving husband.

ENDYMION PORTER TO HIS WIFE, 1621

Since my coming into Spain I have received four letters from you, and the two first with so much kindness in them, as I thought my love rewarded; but the two last are so full of mistrusts and falsehoods, that I rather fear you have changed your affection than that you have any sure grounds for what you accuse me of in them, for as I hope for mercy at God's hands I neither kist nor touched any woman since I left you, and for the innkeeper's daughter at Boulogne, I was so far from kissing her, that as I hope to be saved I cannot remember that I saw any such woman . . . Good Olive, let me receive no more quarrelling letters from you, for I desire but your love, it being the thing that only affords me pleasure in this vile world. Send me word how the children do, and whether Charles [their second son] be black or fair, and who he is like.

ENDYMION PORTER TO HIS WIFE, 1624

My dear Wife and Children, My love, which neither sea, nor land, nor death can extinguish towards you, most endearedly visits you with eternal embraces, and will abide with you for ever. My dear wife, remember thou was the love of my youth and the joy of my life, the most beloved, as well as most worthy of all my earthly comforts. God knows and thou knowest it, it was a match of Providence's own making . . .

And now, dear children, be obedient to your dear mother, whose virtue and good name is an honour to you, for she hath been exceeded by none in integrity, industry, and virtue, and good understanding . . .

Yours as God pleaseth, which no waters can quench, no time forget, nor distance wear away, but remains for ever.

WILLIAM PENN TO HIS FAMILY, 4 June 1682 ON THE EVE OF
HIS DEPARTURE FOR AMERICA

My dearest friend, thou adducest my leaving thee to follow the call of my profession, as a poor proof of my affection for thee. Dost thou not know, my beloved, that we could have barely existed in England? That both thou and me must have been debarred of even necessaries: unless we had given up our independence to have procured them from perhaps unwilling friends. It was only upon the certainty of obtaining an employment, the produce of which would be adequate to thy support as well as my own, that I dared to follow the wishes of my heart and press thee to be mine. Heaven knows with what sincerity and warmth of affection I have loved thee – how anxiously I look forward to the time when I may return to thee, and how earnestly I labour that the delight of our meeting may be no more clouded with the fear of a long parting. Do not then, my beloved, adduce the following of the dictates of necessity as my crime . . . Let not unavailing sorrow increase thy malady, but look my dear Ann to the happy side. See me engaged, successfully thus far, in the cause of science and followed by the good wishes and approbation of the world.

MATTHEW FLINDERS TO HIS WIFE, ANN, 7 JANUARY 1802

Goody, Goody, Dear Goody, You said you would weary, and I do hope in my heart you are wearying. It will be so sweet to make it all up to you in kisses when I return. You will *take me* and hear all my bits of experiences, and your heart will beat when you find how I have longed to return to you. Darling, dearest, loveliest, 'The Lord bless you.' I think of you every hour, every moment. I love you and admire you, like – like anything. My own Good-Good . . .

Dearest, I wonder if you are getting any victual. There must be cocks at least, and the chickens will surely have laid their eggs. I have many an anxious thought about you: and I wonder if you sleep at nights, or if you are wandering about – on, on – smoking and killing mice. Oh, if I was there I could put my arms so close about your neck, and hush you into the softest sleep you have had since I went away. Good night. Dream of me.

> I am ever,
> Your own Goody
> JANE WELSH CARLYLE TO HER HUSBAND,
> 30 DECEMBER 1828

Alas! and I have no soft Aladdin's Palace here to bid you hasten and take repose in. Nothing but a noisy, untoward lodging-house, and no better shelter than my own bosom. Yet is not this the best of all shelters for you? the only safe place in this wide world? Thank God, this still is yours, and I can receive you there without distrust, and wrap you close with the solacements of a true heart's love. Hasten thither, then, my own wife. Betide what may, we will not despair, were the world never so unfriendly. *We* are indivisible, and will help each other to endure its evils, nay to conquer them.

> THOMAS CARLYLE, TO HIS WIFE, JANE,
> 12 SEPTEMBER 1831

Weddings

The marriage of Jane and Thomas Carlyle was not entirely happy:

> It was very good of God to let Carlyle and Mrs Carlyle marry one another and so make only two people miserable instead of four.
>
> SAMUEL BUTLER

Never was a man more fortunate in his wife than I, never a wife more loving, tender, delicious, yet with it all, clear and level headed. Your letter was like an exquisite soft warm breeze of spring in this lonely desert . . . More than once I have taken myself to task for my folly in leaving such a wife and baby (babies now) for this work. But there is something beyond me, something outside of me, which impels me irresistibly to the work. I shall certainly come back to you, then hand in hand we will meet the days and years until the end comes.

ROBERT PEARY, TO HIS WIFE, JOSEPHINE, 27 AUGUST 1899

Dearest Bunny,

Do you know what this is – a wedding anniversary letter. I think it should arrive about on the right date. Do you remember that hot June day thirty-three years ago? – the church jammed – Father with a lovely waistcoat with small blue spots – the Rough Riders – the ushers in cutaways – the crowds in the street – your long white veil and tight little bodice – the reception at Aunt Harriet's – Uncle Ed – your mother with one of her extraordinary hats that stood straight up.

And do you remember what the world was then – little and cozy – a different order of things, wars considered on the basis of a Dick [Richard Harding] Davis novel, a sort of 'As it was in the beginning' atmosphere over life. We've come a long way down a strange road since then. Nothing has happened as we imagined it would except our children. We never thought we'd roam the world. We never thought our occupations and interests would cover such a range. We never thought that our thirty-third anniversary would find us deep in our second war and me again at the front. Well, darling, we've lived up to the most important part of the ceremony, 'In sickness and in health, for richer for poorer, till death do you part.'

THEODORE ROOSEVELT, JR., TO HIS WIFE, ELEANOR (BUNNY)
20 MAY 1943

My sweet beloved Winston, I am so happy with you my Dear. You have so transformed my life that I can hardly remember what it felt like three years ago before I knew you.

CLEMENTINE CHURCHILL TO HER HUSBAND, WINSTON, 1911

For seven years you have filled my whole life and now I feel more than half my life has vanished across the channel . . .

CLEMENTINE CHURCHILL TO HER HUSBAND, WINSTON,
NOVEMBER 1915

Oh my Darling, I'm thinking so much of you and how you have enriched my life. I have loved you very much but I wish I had been a more amusing wife to you. How nice it would be if we were both young again.

CLEMENTINE CHURCHILL TO HER HUSBAND, WINSTON,
1 JANUARY 1935 (THEY HAD BEEN MARRIED FOR TWENTY-SEVEN
YEARS)

My darling Clemmie,

In your letter from Madras you wrote some words vy dear to me, about my having enriched yr life. I cannot tell you what pleasure this gave me, because I always feel so overwelmingly in yr debt, if there can be accounts in love. It was sweet of you to write this to me, and I hope and pray I shall be able to make you happy and secure during my remaining years, and cherish you my darling one as you deserve, and leave you in comfort when my race is run. What it has been to me to live all these years in yr heart and companionship no phrases can convey. Time passes swiftly, but is it not joyous to see how great and growing is the treasure we have gathered together, amid the storms and stresses of so many eventful and to millions tragic and terrible years? . . .

WINSTON CHURCHILL TO HIS WIFE, CLEMENTINE,
23 JANUARY 1935

Children

My other dear daughter was this day married at Christchurch, St Marylebone, to the Rev. Lewis Playters Hird. I never felt anything more acutely than parting from this dear child, and may God be a Father to her wherever she goes. My family are now all disposed of, and I remain as the mere scaffold on which has for more than twenty years been building, as it were, the edifice of their education.

COLONEL PETER HAWKER

We had no children and at first this was a sadness, partly because all my friends were having babies and I was left out. But we got used to being childless and I am now increasingly grateful that we did not have a family because although I know Reggie would have been a wonderful father and grandfather, I think I might have been a bossy nagger of a mother. I would quite like to have been a grandmother, but then that's not a difficult thing to be – all the pleasure and little of the responsibility. Looking round at the couples we know who have *remained* consistently happily married I note that many are childless. Of course it is possible to rationalise anything, and may be that is what I am doing, but I believe there is some truth in what I am saying. Compensating could be a part of it? Perhaps, but it looks to me as if childless couples who are truly devoted find fulfilment without the accepted necessity of dividing allegiance and are not to be pitied.

JOYCE GRENFELL

Women have to bear the stress of [the] lapse of energies even more than men; to an exciting girlhood succeeds marriage, the fierce joys and preoccupations of mother-hood, the sympathetic handling of the varying dispositions of the growing family; then the launching away of the little ships begins; the boys settle down to work in the world, the girls marry; and quite suddenly, sometimes, the wheels stop working, and the mother, whose life has been so full of others' cares, finds herself in a moment with nothing what-ever to do but to manage a house, and to devote herself to her husband, whose interests in many cases have been rather thrust into the shade by the life and problems of the children.

A. C. BENSON, *ALONG THE ROAD*

Every gardener prunes the roots of a tree before it is transplanted, but no one had ever pruned me. If you have been sunned through and through like an apricot on a wall from your earliest days, you are over-sensitive to any with-drawal of heat. This had been clearly foreseen by my friends and they were genuinely anxious about the happiness of my stepchildren. I do not know which of us had been considered the boldest in our marriage, my husband or myself; and no doubt step-relationships should not be taken in hand unadvisedly, lightly or wantonly, but reverently, discreetly and soberly.

MARGOT ASQUITH

Oscar Wilde said, 'Children begin by loving their parents; after a time they judge them; rarely, if ever, do they forgive them.' I don't mind the loving and the judging, but, like most mothers, I'd fear lack of forgiveness.

My four-year-old daughter Rosie is holding on to my coat as I try to leave for work. I gently prise her fingers free. 'Mummy has to go now,' I say. 'I don't want you to go. I want you to stay with me,' she sobs. I go with sinking heart. What am I doing with this precious child? My heart's blood. Should I give up work and the family take an income cut? I ring the nanny when I arrive at the office, just ten minutes away, and hear Rosie chuckling in the background with friends. She's too busy to come to the phone.

Still I worry. Working mothers – and that's about 63 per cent of women in this country – are so much the butt of criticism at present. We are portrayed as selfish harpies who leave our offspring without a backward glance so that we can feel self-important and buy a new fridge. Some say we are a threat to the nation's future – our absence will cause a generation of children to grow up maladjusted and antisocial.

The fact that most mothers work not simply for self-fulfilment but because families need incomes is ignored. So is the widespread problem of job insecurity. If others give up work, may not this put a terrible burden on a husband's shoulders – that if he stumbles the whole edifice can come down?

I say to my 18-year-old son Thomas, rather pathetically, 'Do you think I harmed you by being a working mother?'

'God no, Mum,' he says. 'The last thing any of us want round our necks is a mother who doesn't work, asking questions all the time about where we've been. You do that anyway,' he adds kindly. 'And I didn't feel so bad when I left to go to university because I knew you'd got something to do. The worst problems my friends had were with mothers who didn't work crying all the time before they left. They could hardly wait to get out of it.'

Well, actually, I cried all the way back from Oxford . . .

Mothers can never get it absolutely right. Criticised for not leaving, for leaving, for showing too much interest, too little, we try valiantly to provide what is required of us. And the requirement keeps changing. But then, the whole point of this raging love is that it's not intended to create perfection, just to see to it that the next generation of the human race is raised more or less intact. And there are a lot of different ways of doing it . . .

'The great thing about mothers is that you can blame them for all sorts of your own misbehaviour,' Thomas grins, as he packs up to go back to university. 'So don't keep on about me eating properly and working hard. Just stop it, or I'll ring you up and tell you I'm taking drugs and you've driven me to it. Don't worry,' he says, kissing me. 'Honestly, I'm fine. You're fine. Actually, you're great.'

And he walks away from me, down the pavement, tall, handsome, happy, without turning round.

And not mine any more.

KATHARINE HADLEY IN YOU MAGAZINE, 23 FEBRUARY 1997

Our three children were all married during the years of [my husband's] illness, and it was then that I most missed his wisdom and support. Sophie and Robert Gore came first in February 1976. It was a day flooded with the love and friendship of their many friends. We had little tables spread for dinner in all the rooms of the house which somehow seemed to expand with its welcoming candlelight.

Then it seemed but a few weeks later that Lucy, with a radiant face, asked if we could manage another wedding in the autumn, as she and Mark Le Fanu had decided 'to take the plunge'. It transpired that they wanted a marquee, and an evening dance, and about fifty people to stay. My heart sank; how to do this after having already had so much hospitality from our neighbours for Sophie's wedding. But Hawkwood College . . . happened to be empty for just that one night. When The Day came, friends flowed in and out of Over Court continuously. The marquee was great, and we danced through the night even through a torrential storm – or rather 'they' did, for I spent much of the night taking off my long evening skirt unblocking the flooding drains.

JW [author's son] and Elizabeth Hindmarsh were married three years later in the Inner Temple Church in London, where Elizabeth had her 'chambers' as a practising barrister, and JD came to the party in a wheelchair. The singing of the famous choir and the beauty of the ancient church are still vivid memories. Then we sat down to a splendid luncheon in the Great Hall, and walked the lawns in golden July sunshine, before the happy pair rattled off in JW's open Morgan sports car amid our cheers and good wishes.

RHODA COWEN, *THE GOLD AND SILVER THREADS: A MEMOIR OF LIFE IN THE TWENTIETH CENTURY*

And a woman who held a babe against her bosom said,
    Speak to us of Children.
    And he said:
    Your children are not your children.
    They are the sons and daughters of Life's longing for
        itself.

Marriage

They come through you but not from you,
And though they are with you yet they belong not to
    you.

You may give them your love but not your thoughts,
For they have their own thoughts.
You may house their bodies but not their souls,
For their souls dwell in the house of to-morrow, which
    you cannot visit, not even in your dreams.
You may strive to be like them, but seek not to make
    them like you.
For life goes not backward nor tarries with yesterday.
You are the bows from which your children as living
    arrows are sent forth.

The archer sees the mark upon the path of the infinite,
    and He bends you with His might that His arrows
    may go swift and far.
Let your bending in the Archer's hand be for gladness;
For even as He loves the arrow that flies, so He loves
    also the bow that is stable.

KAHLIL GIBRAN, THE PROPHET

Thankfulness

This day, whate'er the Fates decree,
Shall still be kept with joy by me:
This day then, let us not be told,
That you are sick, and I grown old,
Nor think on our approaching ills,
And talk of spectacles and pills;
To morrow will be time enough
To hear such mortifying stuff.

Although we now can form no more
Long schemes of life, as heretofore;
Yet you, while time is running fast,
Can look with joy on what is past.

. . .

Does not the body thrive and grow
By food of twenty years ago?
And, had it not been still supplied,
It must a thousand times have died.
Then, who with reason can maintain,
That no effects of food remain?
And, is not virtue in mankind
The nutriment that feeds the mind?
Upheld by each good action past,
And still continued by the last:
Then, who with reason can pretend,
That all effects of virtue end?

. . .

O then, whatever heav'n intends,
Take pity on your pitying friends;
Nor let your ills affect your mind,
To fancy they can be unkind.
Me, surely me, you ought to spare,
Who gladly would your suff'rings share;
Or give my scrap of life to you,
And think it far beneath your due;
You, to whose care so oft I owe,
That I'm alive to tell you so.

JONATHAN SWIFT

How very fortunate are those few who in the Person they love, meet with the principles of Honour and Virtue to guide them through the World, but this, my fortune, so happy and so rare, shall not breed in me that insolence of opinion that I deserve it, but I will still look up to Heaven and you with gratitude and continual acknowledgements.

LETTER FROM ELIZABETH MONTAGU TO HER HUSBAND, 1742

You have ever been my Pride, I have loved and honoured you with the tenderest affection, and will continue to do so as long as I live, but I now adore you for the greatness of mind, joined with the utmost regard shewn to me in a letter which might have well become a Roman Lady. The happiest days that I ever past in my life, have been with you, and I hope Heaven, after these storms shall be blown over, will grant me the long enjoyment of your charming society, which I prefer above everything upon Earth.

FROM A LETTER FROM EDWARD MONTAGU TO HIS WIFE, 1745

Here ends the best & brightest & most blessed year of my life. It is as tho' I had reached the goal of my boy-existence & found it but the starting post of a new one. The mountain tops before me show higher than ever & life is become a more earnest business with a larger sphere & higher pleasures & deeper responsibilities – no longer alone but blest with the companionship of a noble & pure spirit, with the possession of a deeply loving heart; how abundantly grateful ought mine to be!

BARCLAY FOX, 31 DECEMBER 1844 (HE HAD MARRIED JANE BACKHOUSE)

During the first ten years of our married life we were always in debt. Only by exercising the greatest care, were we able, at the best of times, to get both ends within a penny of meeting; and often enough Nell and I have looked up from our work on the Budget with something like hopelessness in our eyes. It was so hard. Neither of us cared for money in itself. We wanted only enough, or nearly enough, to maintain life decently . . .

We had the gift of hope. We saw more sunshine than gloom in the world. We knew, we saw, that around us were thousands in worse condition than ourselves. We felt that for many things we had cause for thankfulness. Health was ours, and youth, and content. Yes, content. The worst was past. The future held promise. Here in the living present was our home, our own, the children in it and ourselves. We were quite happy there. To see and hear us, you might have thought we had never a care, hardly a want.

S. F. BULLOCK, QUOTED IN DONALD READ, '*DOCUMENTS FROM EDWARDIAN ENGLAND*'

It was at Gray's that I met the prettiest girl I had seen in my life. She was blonde, with huge eyes, and her name was Christine. She had come on a tentative expedition with friends from Muswell Hill, which was considered a rather upper-class area by our standards.

I knew she was my girl straight away. I nearly had a brawl with another bloke who also liked her. He was quite good-looking and kept taunting me: 'I can have her any time.' He didn't. I wound up with her and I found she was a lovely girl . . . I persuaded her that I loved her, and I became her steady boyfriend.

In those days there was a firmly set out path for a young man to follow. First he got the violence out of his system, then he went out with a girl for a two-year period before he married her and settled down. To my surprise, Christine's parents accepted me as her regular chap . . .

Christine was working in an office in Bond Street and we used to meet for lunch most days in Lyons Corner House, like Trevor Howard and Celia Johnson in *Brief Encounter*. We started making plans to marry over an economy bowl of soup and a roll.

. . . my mother was able to buy the house where we lived, and shortly afterwards to sell it again . . . Before leaving she made arrangements for me to rent the top two floors, and Christine and I were married.

It was not the most stylish occasion. How uncomfortable and conspicuous we felt in our new clothes as we left Liverpool Street station in a train taking a crowd of soldiers back to barracks in Colchester, and us to an unimaginative honeymoon on the East Coast. When we returned to our fifty-shillings-a-week flat I put up some wallpaper and magnolia gloss, which I thought took Fonthill Road upmarket a bit, and decked out one room to serve as darkroom, kitchen and bathroom. The tin bath was kept by the stove, to be handy for transferring hot water. All we had besides were a few sticks of furniture and a dubious television; a visitor would get the chair while we sat on the bed . . .

For me, the real decision to live dangerously was taken in Paris, where I had gone with Christine to make up for our mundane honeymoon. Paris, after all, was the home of serious photo-journalism, with *Paris-Match* and the great agencies like Magnum, and so Paris could not be ignored if I was at all serious about my work. It all started with a Frenchman making a pass at my very pretty wife and receiving from me – as he would have done at Gray's Academy in Finsbury Park – the offer of my fist and a mouthful of obscene threats, incomprehensible as they were to him. The scene reduced my poor wife to tears, and afterwards we sat in a cafe while I leafed glumly through the magazines . . . It was the beginning of the Berlin crisis and the Wall. Suddenly I saw the direction in which my photography had to go. I said out loud: 'I have absolutely GOT to go to Berlin.'

She did not even flinch or complain, that wife of mine. Indeed I owe her an enormous debt of gratitude for encouraging my ideas. She always supported me – although she had no inkling as yet of how much her tolerance would be expected to bear in the coming years as I travelled further and further into danger, when often it must have seemed as if I were trying to commit suicide.

DON MCCULLIN, *UNREASONABLE BEHAVIOUR: AN*
AUTOBIOGRAPHY

Sweet Marabel, the priestess of my soul,
Wife, counsellor, companion of my life
Whose shining wisdom and whose grace console
My dumb frustration's tears at Pyrrhic strife:
See how we journey through the arching years,
As through the rainbows of illumined storms,
And how the thunder-clouds which woke our fears
Are split asunder by ethereal forms.

Let us go down this day in gratitude
To where, years since, our vows were solemnised,
Remembering how in piety we stood
Beyond all hoping 'raptured and surprised:
    Never forget the splendour and the praise
    That glorified us then for future days.

ROLF GARDINER, ON THE TENTH ANNIVERSARY OF THEIR
MARRIAGE

We thank God, then, for the pleasures, joys and triumphs of marriage; for the cups of tea we bring each other, and the seedlings in the garden frame; for the domestic drama of meetings and partings, sickness and recovery; for the grace of occasional extravagance, flowers on birthdays and unexpected presents; for talk at evenings of the events of the day; for the ecstasy of caresses; for gay mockery at each other's follies; for plans and projects, fun and struggle; praying that we may neither neglect nor undervalue these things, nor be tempted to think of them as self-contained and self-sufficient.

SOCIETY OF FRIENDS

Hymns

The following hymns listed in alphabetical order can be found variously in Hymns Ancient & Modern New Standard; Hymns Ancient & Modern Revised; The Anglican Hymn Book (1965) Hymns and Psalms (1983); *and* The New English Hymnal (1986). *These are referred to in the following list respectively as* A&MNS; A&MR; AHB; H&P; NEH. *You will have your own favourites, but you may well wish to refresh your memory of some of these hymns by looking them up and deciding for yourself. The sub-heading 'Music' gives you the composer of the tune and the name of the tune, where known. Many are sung to more than one tune. The tunes will be found in the index to the music editions of the hymn books referred to, one or more of which the church organist will have. You will soon find your favourite.*

Some hymns may be found overlong for the wedding service, e.g. the popular 'All things bright and beautiful', with its repeated chorus. It would be kind to your guests to omit one or two verses. Many hymns will be found to contain verses inappropriate to a wedding. These may often be omitted. The celebrant and church organist can advise.

Alleluya! sing to Jesus! His the Sceptre, His the Throne	A&MNS **262**; A&MR **399**; AHB **383**, H&P **592**, NEH **271** Words: W. Chatterton Dix, 1837–98 Music: R. H. Prichard, 1811–87 *Hyfrydol* S. S. Wesley, 1810–76, *Alleluya*

All creatures of our God and King,
Lift up your voice and with us sing

A&MNS **105**; A&MR **172**; AHB **251**;
 H&P **329**; NEH **263**
Words: St Francis of Assisi, trans. Wm
 Draper, 1855–1933
Music: *Lasst uns Erfreuen* (Geistliche
 Kirchengesang *arr. Vanghan
 Williams, 1872–1958 or* Cölner
 Gesangbuch, 1623)

All my hope on God is founded;
He doth still my trust renew

A&MNS **336**; H&P **63**; NEH **333**
Words: Robert Bridges, 1844–1930
Music: H. Howells, 1892–1983 *Michael*
 Melody J. Neader, Alpha and Omega
 (1680), harmony
 The Chorale Book for England
 (1863) *Meine Hoffnung*

All people that on earth do dwell,
Sing to the Lord with cheerful voice

A&MNS **100**; A&MR **166**; AHB **231**;
 H&P **1**; NEH **334**
Words: W. Kethe d. 1594, Psalm 100
Music: arr. Vaughan Williams, 1872–
 1958 *Old 100th*

All things bright and beautiful
All creatures great and small

A&MNS **116**; A&MR **442**; AHB **233**;
 H&P **330**; NEH **264**
Words: Mrs C. F. Alexander, 1818–95
Music: W. H. Monk, 1823–89, *All
 things bright and beautiful*
 Trad. arr. Martin Shaw, 1875–1958
 Royal Oak

And did those feet in ancient time
Walk upon England's mountains green
(Jerusalem)

A&MNS **254**; A&MR **578**; NEH **488**
Words: William Blake, 1757–1827
Music: C. H. H. Parry, 1848–1918
 Jerusalem

As man and woman we were made
That love be found and life begun

H&P **364**
Words: Brian A. Wren (b. 1936)
Music: Trad. arr. Vaughan Williams,
 1872–1958 *Sussex Carol*

Blest are the pure in heart,
For they shall see our God

A&MNS **238**; A&MR **335**; AHB **638**;
   H&P **724**; NEH **341**
Words: J. Keble, 1792–1866
Music: W. H. Havergal, 1793–1870
   Franconia

Come down, O Love Divine
Seek thou this soul of mine

A&MNS **156**; A&MR **235**; AHB **214**;
   H&P **281**; NEH **137**
Words: Bianco da Siena (d. 1434)
   trans. R. F. Littledale, 1833–90
Music: R. Vaughan Williams, 1872–
   1958 *Down Ampney*

Come, Holy Ghost, our souls inspire
And lighten with celestial fire

A&MNS **93**; A&MR **157**; AHB **216**;
   H&P **283**; NEH **138**
Words: Bishop J. Cosin, 1594–1672,
   from the Latin
Music: *Veni Creator Spiritus*, mode viii
   Mechlin version

Crown with love, Lord, this glad day
Love to humble and delight.

A&MNS **450**
Words: Ian M. Fraser (b. 1917)

Dear Lord and Father of mankind
Forgive our foolish ways!

A&MNS **115**; A&MR **157**, AHB **608**;
   H&P **673**; NEH **353**
Words: J. G. Whittier, 1807–92
Music: C. H. H. Parry, 1848–1918
   Repton
   F. C. Maker, 1844–1927 *Rest*
   Bernard S. Massey (b. 1927)
   Mansfield College

Eternal Ruler of the ceaseless round
Of circling planets singing on their way

A&MNS **353**; AHB **419**; NEH **355**
Words: J. W. Chadwick, 1840–1904
Music: Orlando Gibbons, 1583–1625
   Song 1

Father, hear the prayer we offer
Not for ease that prayer shall be

A&MNS **113**; A&MR **182**; AHB **579**;
    H&P **436**; NEH **357**
Words: Maria Willis, 1824–1908
Music: J. Stewer, 1668–1761 *Gott Will's*
    Machen
      Trad. arr. Vaughan Williams, 1872–
      1958 Sussex

Father, Lord of all Creation,
Ground of Being, Life and Love

A&MNS **356**
Words: Stewart Cross, 1928–88

Fill thou my life, O Lord my God,
In every part with praise

A&MNS **200**; A&MR **373**; AHB **621**;
    H&P **792**
Words: H. Bonar, 1808–89
Music: *Richmond*
    Henry J. Gauntlet, 1805–76 *St Fulbert*
    J. B. Dykes, 1823–76 *Beatitudo*

For the beauty of the earth
For the beauty of the skies

A&MNS **104**; A&MR **171**; AHB **18**;
    H&P **333**; NEH **285**
Words: F. S. Pierpoint, 1835–1917
Music: Trad. arr. Geoffrey Shaw 1879–
    1943 *England's Lane*
    David Evans, 1874–1948 *Lucerna*
    Laudoniae

Glorious things of thee are spoken,
Sion, city of our God

A&MNS **172**; A&MR **257**; AHB **424**;
    H&P **817**; NEH **362**
Words: John Newton, 1725–1807
Music: Cyril V. Taylor (b. 1907) *Abbot's*
    Leigh
    Franz Joseph Haydn, 1732–1809
    Austria

God of mercy, God of grace,
Show the brightness of thy face

A&MNS **179**; A&MR **264**; AHB **421**;
    NEH **366**
Words: H. Flyte, 1793–1847 Psalm 67
Music: *Heathlands*

God moves in a mysterious way
His wonders to perform

A&MNS **112**; A&MR **181**; AHB **403**;
   H&P **65**; NEH **365**
Words: W. Cowper, 1731–1800
Music: Playford's Psalms, 1671 *London
   New*
   Hymns and Sacred Poems, Dublin
   1749 *Irish*

Guide me, Oh thou great Redeemer
   [Jehovah]
Pilgrim through this barren land

A&MNS **214**; A&MR **296**; AHB **555**;
   H&P **437**; NEH **368**
Words: W. Williams 1717–91
Music: John Hughes, 1873–1932 *Cwm
   Rhondda*

Happy are they, they that love God
Whose hearts have Christ confest

A&MNS **176**; A&MR **261**; AHB **532**;
   H&P **711**; NEH **369**
Words: Robert Bridges, 1844–1930,
   based on Latin of Charles Coffin,
   1676–1749
Music: William Croft, 1678–1727
   Binchester

Happy the home that welcomes you,
   Lord Jesus,
Truest of friends, most honoured guest
   of all

H&P **366**
Words: Karl Johann Philipp Spitta,
   1801–59
   trans. Honor Mary Thwaites (b. 1914)
Music: J. B. Dykes, 1823–76 *Strength
   and Stay*

Hark, my soul, it is the Lord
'Tis thy Saviour, hear his Word

A&MNS **244**; A&MR **344**; AHB **533**;
   H&P **521**
Words: W. Cowper, 1731–1800
Music: J. B. Dykes, 1823–76 *St Bees*
   J. Wesley's *Foundery Collection* 1742
   Herrnhut
   William H. Harris, 1883–1973
   Petersfield

Help us to help each other, Lord,
Each other's cross to bear

A&MNS **374**
Words [Cento from] Charles Wesley,
   1707–88

He who would valiant be 'Gainst all disaster *or* Who would true valour see Let him come hither	A&MNS **212**; A&MR **22**; AHB **587**; H&P **688**; NEH **372** Words: John Bunyan, 1628–88, and others Music: English traditional *Monks Gate*
I danced in the morning when the world was begun, And I danced in the moon and the stars and the sun	A&MNS **375**; NEH **375** Words: Sydney Carter (b. 1915)
I vow to thee, my country – all earthly things above – Entire and whole and perfect, the service of my love	A&MNS **295**; A&MR **579** Words: Sir Cecil Spring-Rice, 1859–1918 Music: Gustav Holst 1874–1934 *Thaxted*
Immortal, invisible, God only wise In light inaccessible hid from our eyes	A&MNS **199**; A&MR **327**; AHB **242**; H&P **9**; NEH **377** Words: W. Chalmers Smith, 1824–1908 Music: Welsh Hymn Melody *St Denio*

Immortal Love, for ever full
Forever flowing free
	A&MNS **133**; A&MR **208**; AHB **537**;
	H&P **392**; NEH **378**
	Words: J. G. Whittier, 1807–92
	Music: J. Clark, 1673–1707
	   Bishopsthorpe
	   J. Dykes Bower, 1905–81 *Haresfield*
	   C. Hutcheson, 1792–1860 *Stracathro*

In heavenly love abiding
No change my heart shall fear
	AHB **524**; H&P **678**
	Words: Anna L. Waring , 1823–1910
	Music: C. Urban, 1790–1845
	   Rutherford
	   D. Jenkins, 1848–1915 *Penlan*

Jesus, good above all other Gentle child of gentle mother	A&MNS **378**; AHB **263**; H&P **732**; NEH **387** Words: Percy Dearmer, 1867–1936 Music: German ms, 1410 *Quem* *pastores laudavere*

Jesus, Lord, we look to thee,
Let us in thy name agree

A&MNS **380**; AHB **423**; H&P **759**;
  NEH **481**
Words: [Cento from] Charles Wesley,
  1707–88
Music: *Vienna*
  G. F. Handel, 1685–1759 *Theodora*

Jesus, Lord, we pray,
Be our guest today

A&MNS **475**; H&P **365**
Words: Basil E. Bridge (b.1927)
Music: A. Drese, 1620–1701
    Seelenbraütigam
  W. Llewellyn (b. 1925) *Westron*
  Wynde

Jesus, where'er thy people meet,
There they behold thy mercy-seat

A&MNS **162**; A&MR **245**; AHB **8**;
  H&P **549**; NEH **390**
Words: W. Cowper, 1731–1800
Music. T. Turton, 1780–1864 *Ely*
  W. Knapp, 1698–1768 *Wareham*

King of glory, King of peace,
I will love thee

A&MNS **194**; A&MR **367**; AHB **539**;
  H&P **499**; NEH **391**
Words: George Herbert, 1593–1632
Music: J. D. Jones, 1827–70
  Gwalchmai
  J. Wilson (b. 1905) *Bemerton*

Lead us, Heavenly Father, lead us
O'er the world's tempestuous sea

A&MNS **224**; A&MR **311**; AHB **393**;
  H&P **68**; NEH **393**
Words: J. Edmeston, 1791–1867
Music: F. Filitz, 1804–76 *Mannheim*
  E. J. Hopkins, 1818–1901 *Feniton*
  Court

Light's abode, celestial Salem
Vision dear whence peace doth spring

A&MNS **185**; A&MR **279**; AHB **434**;
  NEH **401**
Words: St Thomas à Kempis, *c.* 1379–
  1471 trans. J. M. Neale
Music: H. Smart, 1813–79 *Regent*
  Square

Lord of all good, our gifts we bring to thee;
Use them thy holy purpose to fulfil

A&MNS **393**; H&P **797**
Words: Albert F. Bayly, 1901–84
Music: Erik Routley, 1917–82 *Cliff Town*

Lord of all hopefulness, Lord of all joy
Whose trust, ever child-like, no cares could destroy

A&MNS **294**; H&P **552**; NEH **239**
Words: Jan Struther, 1901–53
Music: Irish traditional *Slane*
    Cyril V. Taylor (b. 1907) *Miniver*

Lord of the home, your only Son
Received a mother's tender love

H&P **367**
Words: Albert F. Bayly, 1901–84
Music: A. E. Floyd, 1877–1974 *Vermont*

Lord, thy Word abideth
And our footsteps guideth

A&MNS **166**; A&MR **250**; AHB **305**;
    H&P **476**; NEH **407**
Words: Sir H. W. Baker, 1821–77
Music: arr. W. H. Monk *Ravenshaw*
    (Weisse's Gesangbuch, 1531)

Lord, you give to us the precious gift of life
A stewardship for every husband, every wife

H&P **368**
Words: Stephen Orchard (b. 1942)
Music: John Wilson (b. 1905)
    Binscombe

Love divine, all loves excelling,
Joy of heaven, to earth come down

A&MNS **131**; A&MR **205**; AHB **625**;
    H&P **267**; NEH **408**
Words: Charles Wesley, 1707–88
Music: J. Stainer, 1840–1901 *Love divine*
    W. Rowlands, 1860–1937 *Blaenwern*
    J. Wesley's *Sacred Harmony* 1780
    Westminster

Loving shepherd of thy sheep
Keep thy lamb, in safety keep

A&MNS **134**; A&MR **444**; AHB **337**
Words: Jane E. Leeson, 1807–82
Music: L. G. Hayne, 1836–83 *Buckland*

My soul, there is a country
Far beyond the stars

A&MNS **191**; A&MR **286**; NEH **412**
Words: Henry Vaughan, 1622–95
Music: Melchior Vulpius, 1560–1616
    Christus der ist Mein Leben

Now thank we all our God
With heart and hands and voices

A&MNS **205**; A&MR **379**; AHB **22**;
  H&P **566**; NEH **413**
Words: M. Rinkart, 1586–1649, trans.
  C. Winkworth
Music: J. Cruger, 1598–1662 *Nun*
  Danket
  I. A. Copley (b. 1926) *Falmer*

O Father all creating,
Whose wisdom love and power

AHB **391**
Words: J. Ellerton, 1876
Music: *Dies Dominica*

Of all the Spirit's gifts to me
I pray that I may never cease

A&MNS **503**; H&P **320**
Words: F. Pratt Green (b. 1903)
Music: Norman Cocker, 1889–1953
  Ripponden

O God, our help in ages past,
Our hope for years to come

A&MNS **99**; A&MR **165**; AHB **244**;
H&P **358**; NEH **417**
Words: I. Watts, 1674–1748
Music: William Croft, 1678–1727
  St Anne

O God, whose loving hand has led
Thy children to this joyful day

NEH **319**
Words: John Boyd Moore

O Holy Spirit, Lord of grace,
Eternal fount of love

A&MNS **152**; A&MR **231**; AHB **291**;
  H&P **310**; NEH **419**
Words: John Chandler, 1808–76 from
  the Latin of Charles Coffin, 1676–
  1749
Music: Thomas Tallis, c. 1505–85
  Tallis' Ordinal

O Perfect love, all human thought
  transcending
Lowly we kneel in prayer before thy
  throne

A&MNS **280**; A&MR **463**; AHB **393**;
  H&P **370**; NEH **320**
Words: Dorothy F. Gurney, 1858–1932
Music: *Strength and Stay*
  J. Barnby, 1838–1906 *O Perfect Love*

O praise ye the Lord! praise him in
  the height:
Rejoice in his word, ye angels of light

A&MNS **203**; A&MR **376**; AHB **23**;
  NEH **427**
Words: H. W. Baker, 1821–77 based on
  Psalm 150
Music: *Laudate dominum*

O thou who camest from above
The fire celestial to impart

A&MNS **233**; A&MR **329**; AHB **366**;
  H&P **745**; NEH **431**
Words: Charles Wesley, 1707–88
  Leviticus 6:13
Music: S. S. Wesley, 1810–76 *Hereford*
  Samuel Stanley 1767–1822 *Wilton*

Our Father, by whose name
All parenthood is known

H&P **371**
Words: F. Bland Tucker, 1895–1984
Music: J. D. Edwards, 1805–85
  Rhosymedre

O worship the King all glorious above;
O gratefully sing his power and his love

A&MNS **101**; A&MR **167**; AHB **248**;
  H&P **28**; NEH **433**
Words: Robert Grant, 1779–1838
  Psalm 104
Music: William Croft, 1678–1727
  Hanover

Praise, my soul, the King of Heaven,
To his feet thy tribute bring.

A&MNS **192**; A&MR **365**; AHB **247**;
  H&P **13**; NEH **436**
Words: H. F. Lyte, 1793–1847
Music: J. Goss, 1800–80 *Praise my soul*
  Henry Smart, 1813–79 *Regent
  Square*

Praise the Lord! ye heavens, adore him;
Praise him, angels, in the height

A&MNS **195**; A&MR **368**; AHB **29**;
  H&P **15**; NEH **437**
Words: Foundling Hospital Collection
  1796
Music: Franz Joseph Haydn, 1732–
  1809 *Austria*
  Richard Redhead, 1820–1901 *Laus
  Deo*

Praise to the Lord, the Almighty, the King of Creation;
O my soul, praise him, for he is thy health and salvation

A&MNS **207**; A&MR **382**; AHB **246**; H&P **16**; NEH **440**

Words: J. Neander, 1650–80
trans. Catherine Winkworth, 1827–78

Music: *Lobe den Herren* or *Hast du denn, Jesu* (Stralsund Gesangbuch, 1665)

Rejoice, the Lord is King,
Your Lord and King adore

A&MNS **139**; A&MR **216**; AHB **210**; H&P **243**; NEH **443**

Words: Charles Wesley, 1707–88

Music: G. F. Handel, 1685–1759
Gopsal
J. Darwall, 1731–89 *Darwall's 148th*

Teach me, my God and King
In all things thee to see

A&MNS **240**; A&MR **337**; AHB **603**; H&P **803**; NEH **456**

Words: G. Herbert, 1593–1632

Music: English traditional *Sandys*

The grace of life is theirs
Who on this wedding day

H&P **373**

Words: F. Pratt Green (b. 1903)

Music: John Ireland, 1879–1962 *Love Unknown*

The King of love my Shepherd is,
Whose goodness faileth never

A&MNS **126**; A&MR **197**; AHB **546**; H&P **69**; NEH **457**

Words: Sir H. W. Baker, 1821–77

Music: Ancient Irish Hymn Melody *St Columba*
J. B. Dykes, 1823–76 *Dominus regit me*
B. R. Hoare (b. 1935) *Cliff Lane*

The Lord's my Shepherd, I'll not want;
He makes me down to lie

A&MNS **426**; AHB **511**; H&P **70**; NEH **459**

Words: Scottish Psalter 1650

Music: J. Irvine, 1836–87 *Crimond*
Brother James' Air

The Lord my pasture shall prepare
And feed me with a Shepherd's care

A&MNS **111**; A&MR **179**; NEH **458**
Words: Joseph Addison, 1672–1719
Music: H. Carey, *c*. 1690–1743 *Surrey*

The spacious firmament on high
With all the blue ethereal sky

A&MNS **103**; A&MR **170**; AHB **232**;
   H&P **339**; NEH **267**
Words: J. Addison, 1672–1719
Music: E. J. Hopkins, 1818–1901
   Creation
   J. Sheeles, 1688–1761 *London* (or
   Addison's)
   Sir H. Walford Davies, 1869–1941
   Firmament

Thine for ever! God of love,
Hear us from thy throne above

A&MNS **234**; A&MR **330**; AHB **364**;
   NEH **463**
Words: Mrs M. F. Maude, 1820–1913
Music: W. Maclagan, 1826–1910
   Newington

Thou God of truth and love,
We seek thy perfect way

H&P **374**
Words: Charles Wesley, 1707–88
Music: J. B. Dykes, 1823–1876 *St
   Godric*

We lift our hearts, O Father,
To Thee our voices raise

AHB **392**
Words: E. A. Welch 1889
Music: *Christus der ist mein Leben*

Music

The principal opportunities for music at your wedding are at the Entrance of the Bride, during the signing of the register, and the Recessional when the newly-weds and close family members process down the aisle and out of the church. The following are merely suggestions. You probably have your own favourite pieces of music from which you would wish to choose; you will certainly know one that is a favourite of yours. You can have your choice played at the service (CD or cassette tape) by arrangement with the celebrant. Your local Public Library should have a copy of The Gramophone: Classical Catalogue (Master Edition), *which will help you to locate the recordings.*

We have not included any modern popular music since the choice is so broad and the couple getting married will no doubt have their special pieces.

You should remember that the parish priest is not only responsible for the worship in his church, he is also responsible for the music. You should discuss your choice of music with the celebrant beforehand. The church organist or choir master will have their own repertoire with which they may feel most comfortable, and you should talk to them as well.

Music

Before the Entrance of the Bride

BACH	*Sheep may safely graze, Cantata No. 208, No. 9*
BRAHMS	*Theme* from the *St Anthony Chorale*
CHARPENTIER	*Prelude to a Te Deum*
CLARKE	*Prince of Denmark's March*
ELGAR	*Nimrod,* from the *Enigma Variations*
GUILMANT	*March* on *Lift up your Heads*
HANDEL	*Hornpipe in D* from the *Water Music*
HANDEL	*March* from *Scipio*
HANDEL	*Coro* from the *Water Music*
HANDEL	*Minuet No. 2* from the *Water Music*
HANDEL	*Organ Concerto in F*
HANDEL	*Arrival of the Queen of Sheba*
HANDEL	*March* from the *Occasional Oratorio*
HARRIS	*Wedding Processional*
HOLLINS	*A Trumpet Minuet*
MONTEVERDI	*Adoramus* and *Cantate Domine*
PARRY	*Bridal March*
PURCELL	*Trumpet Tune* and *Air*
PURCELL	*Rondau* from *Abdelazar*
STANLEY	*Suite in D*
VERDI	*Grand March* from *Aida*
WAGNER	*Bridal March* from *Lohengrin*
WALTON	*March* from *Richard III*
WALTON	*Crown Imperial*
WARLOCK	*Capriol Suite*

The Entrance of the Bride (Processional)

BEETHOVEN	*Hallelujah Chorus* from *The Mount of Olives*
BLISS	*A Wedding Fanfare*
BOYCE	*Trumpet Voluntary*
BRAHMS	*Theme* from the *St Anthony Chorale*
BRIDE	*Allegro Marzialle*

CLARKE	*Trumpet tune*
GUILMANT	*Allegro* from *Sonata in D minor*
HANDEL	*Arrival of the Queen of Sheba*
KARG-ELERT	*Praise the Lord O My Soul*
MENDELSSOHN	*Sonata No. 3, first movement*
MOZART	*Wedding March* from *The Marriage of Figaro*
PURCELL	*Fanfare*
SAINT-SAENS	*Opening of 4th Movement* from *3rd (Organ) Symphony*
STANLEY	*Trumpet Voluntary* from *Suite in D*
SUTTLE	*Wedding March*
WESLEY	*Choral Song*

The Signing of the Register

ALBINONI	*Adagio in G Minor*
ALBINONI	From *Concerto No. 2 in D Minor*
BACH	*Air on a G String*
BACH arr. GOUNOD	*Ave Maria*
BACH	*Jesu, Joy of Man's Desiring*
BACH	*Prelude in E flat*
BRAHMS	*Behold, A Rose is Blooming*
DOWLAND	*Come Again, Sweet Love Doth Now Invite*
DOWLAND	*Now Cease My Wand'ring Eyes*
HANDEL	*Minuet* from *Berenice*
HANDEL	*Air* from the *Water Music*
HANDEL	*Where'er You Walk*
HOLLINS	*Melody*
IRELAND	*Intrada*
MACDOWELL	*To a Wild Rose*
MENDELSSOHN	*Allegretto* from *Sonata No. 4*
MOZART	*Romanze* from *Eine Kleine Nachtmusik*
PALESTRINA	*Sanctus* and *Agnus Dei* from *Missa Brevis*
PARRY	*My Soul, There is a Country*
REDFORD	*Rejoice in the Lord Alway*

SAINT-SAENS	*Benediction Nuptiale*
SCHUBERT	*Ave Maria*
SCHUMANN	*Traumerei*
STANFORD	*Beati quorum via integra est*
VAUGHAN WILLIAMS	*Chorale Prelude on Rhosymedre*
VIVALDI	*Gloria*
WEELKES	*Hosannah to the Son of David*
WESLEY	*Air* from *Three Pieces*

The Bride and Groom Leave the Church (Recessional)

DUBOIS	*Toccata in G*
ELGAR	*Pomp and Circumstance March No. 4*
FLETCHER	*Festive Toccata*
GUILMANT	*Grand Choeur in D*
HOLLINS	*Bridal March*
KARG-ELERT	*Nun Danket Alle Gott*
MENDELSSOHN	*Wedding March* from *A Midsummer Night's Dream*
MENDELSSOHN	*Carillon-Sortie*
PURCELL	*Wedding March*
SMART	*Postlude in D*
VIERNE	*Carillon in B flat*
VIERNE	*Finale* from *Symphony No. 1*
WAGNER	*Wedding March* from *Lohengrin*
WALTON	*Crown Imperial*
WHITLOCK	*Fanfare*
WIDOR	*Toccata* from *Symphony No. 5*

During the Service

There will be congregational singing during the service, certainly of hymns and possibly of a psalm. It will make an enormous difference to the vigour and joyfulness of the wedding if you have a choir to lead the singing and to sing any choral music that you may choose as part of the service. If the church has no choir, you could employ between four and six experienced choral singers to be your choir for the occasion. In relation to the cost of the wedding, this represents a very modest additional sum, between £100 and £250 depending on the number of singers, the location and whether or not the service is to be recorded.

Further Reading

We have examined many wedding guides and books about marriage, and found that the following were the most useful:

Weddings, Collins Gem (The Diagram Group, HarperCollins)

Regina Barreca, *Perfect Husbands (and Other Fairy Tales)* (Harmony Books)

Michael and Myrtle Baughen, *Your Marriage* (Hodder and Stoughton)

Anthony Clare, *Lovelaw: Love, Sex and Marriage Around the World* (BBC Publications)

Erich Fromm, *The Art of Loving* (Unwin paperbacks)

Jacqueline Llewelyn, *Debrett's Wedding Guide*

Kevin Mayhew, *Your Wedding in the Church of England* (Kevin Mayhew Ltd)

Robin Skynner, *One Flesh; Separate Persons* (Constable)

Walter Trobisch, *I Married You* (Inter-Varsity Press)

Helen Wilkinson, *The Proposal: Giving Marriage Back to the People* (Demos Project Report, 1997)

Useful Addresses

For information on wedding services, clerical or civil:

Baptist Union
Baptist House
129 The Broadway
Didcot
Oxon OX11 8RT

The British Humanist Association
47 Theobalds Road
London WC1X 8SP

Catholic Marriage Advisory Council
Clitherow House
1 Blythe Mews
Blythe Road
London W14 0NW

Church of England Enquiry Centre
Church House
Great Smith Street
Westminster
London SW1P 3NZ

Church of Scotland Department of Communication
Wesley Owens Books
117 George Street
Edinburgh EH2 4YN

General Register Office for Northern Ireland
Oxford House
49–55 Chichester Street
Belfast BT1 4HL

General Register Office for Scotland
New Register House
3 West Register Street
Edinburgh EH1 3YT

Greek Orthodox Church Archdiocese of Thyateira and Great Britain
Administrative Offices
5 Craven Hill
London W2 4EN

Jewish Marriage Council
23 Ravenshurst Avenue
London NW4 4EE

Methodist Church
Westminster Central Hall
Storey's Gate
London SW1 9NH

Register General for England and Wales
Smedley Hydro
Trafalgar Road
Southport
Merseyside PR8 2HH

Register General for Guernsey
The Greffe
Royal Court House
St Peter Port
Guernsey GY1 2PB

Scottish Information Office
New St Andrew's House
St James Centre
Edinburgh EH1 3TD

Superintendent Register for Jersey
States Buildings
Royal Square
St Helier
Jersey

United Reformed Church
86 Tavistock Place
London WC1H 9RT

For pre- and post-marital
  guidance:

Marriage Care
Clitherow House
1 Blythe Mews
Blythe Road
London W14 0NW

One Plus One
14 Theobalds Road
London WC1X 8PF

**Relate National Marriage
  Guidance**
Herbert Gray College
Little Church Street
Rugby CV21 3AP

Index of Authors

Index of First Lines

Index of First Lines

Acknowledgments

While every effort has been made to contact owners of copyright material, there are some who have not been traced, and the authors and publishers, who gratefully acknowledge the following copyright owners whose material appears in this book with their permission, would welcome information that will enable them to put matters right when this book is reprinted.

Extracts from The Marriage Service from *The Alternative Service Book 1980* are copyright © The Central Board of Finance of the Church of England and are reproduced by permission;

extracts from *Perfect Husbands* by Regina Barreca Copyright © 1993 by Regina Barreca. Reprinted by permission of Harmony Books, a division of Crown Publishers, Inc.;

extract from 'Marriage: why do we still bother?' by Geraldine Bedell (*Independent on Sunday* 18 August 1996) by kind permission of the Independent;

extract from 'When a Marriage Collapses' by Vanessa Berridge (*Sainsbury's Magazine* March 1997) by kind permission of the author;

Acknowledgments

'In summer wind the elm leaves sing . . .' by John Betjeman quoted in *John Betjeman Letters* Vol. 2 ed. Candida Lycett Green by permission of Methuen London;

extract from 'Love in a Valley' by John Betjeman from *Collected Poems* published by John Murray (Publishers) Ltd by permission of the publishers;

extracts from the Authorized Version of the Bible (the King James Bible) and from the Book of Common Prayer, the rights in which are vested in the Crown, are reproduced by permission of the Crown's patentee, Cambridge University Press;

scripture quotations taken from THE HOLY BIBLE, NEW INTERNATIONAL VERSION Copyright © 1973, 1978, 1984 by International Bible Society. Used by permission of Hodder & Stoughton Limited, a member of the Hodder Headline plc Group. All rights reserved;

extracts from 'Don't Worry, Be Happy' by Fenella Willis, 'Solving Arguments' by Jennie James, and 'A Word of Advice' by Maureen Lipman published in *Brides and Setting Up Home*, July/August 1995, May/June 1996, © Condé Nast PL/Brides and Setting Up by permission of Condé Nast Publications Ltd;

the *Observer* for permission to quote from 'The Loyal Family' by Marina Cantacuzino (19 January 1997) Observer © 1997;

extracts from *Clementine Churchill* by Mary Soames with permission of Curtis Brown Ltd, London, on behalf of Mary Soames Copyright © Mary Soames;

letter to Clementine Churchill dated January 23 1935 reproduced with permission of Curtis Brown Ltd, London, on behalf of The Estate of Sir Winston S. Churchill. Copyright Winston S. Churchill;

extracts from *Lovelaw: Love, Sex and Marriage around the World* by Anthony Clare by permission of A. P. Watt Ltd on behalf of Professor Anthony Clare;

three prayers by Frank Colquhoun from *Family Prayers* (Triangle Books 1984) and *Prayers for Today* (Triangle Books 1989) by permission of SPCK;

extract from *The Noël Coward Diaries* © the Estate of Noël Coward 1982 by kind permission of Alan Brodie Representation Ltd, 211 Piccadilly, London W1V 9LD;

extract from *The Gold and Silver Threads* © 1995 Rhoda Cowen reproduced with the permission of Sutton Publishing Limited, Stroud, Gloucestershire;

extracts from the *Daily Mail*: 'My First Love' by Iris Murdoch (17 August 1996); 'The Secrets of Marriage' by Paul Johnson (8 March 1997); and feature on the Mintel Report (10 May 1997), by permission of Solo Syndication Limited and the Daily Mail

extracts from the *Daily Telegraph*: 'Two Parents are Better' by Janet Daley (29 October 1997) © Janet Daley; and 'Formula for a Lasting Marriage' by Cassandra Jardine (15 November 1996) © Telegraph Group Limited, London, 1996 by permission of Ewan MacNaughton Associates and Telegraph Group Ltd;

extract from *Captain Corelli's Mandolin* by Louis de Bernières by permission of the author and Secker & Warburg Ltd;

extracts from *Love* by Walter de la Mare, by permission of The Literary Trustees of Walter de la Mare, and The Society of Authors as their representative;

thanks to Demos for extracts from their 1997 report, *The Proposal:*

giving marriage back to the people, by Helen Wilkinson (copies available from 9 Bridewell Place, London EC4V 6AP);

'The Double Bubble of Infinity' from *Art & Love* by Kate Farrell. Compilation and Introduction Copyright © 1990 by Kate Farrell, illustrations copyright © 1990 by the Metropolitan Museum of Art. By permission of Little, Brown and Company;

Rosalind Richards as Literary Executor of the Rolf Gardiner Estate for permission to reproduce 'Southwark Cathedral' and an extract from 'Communion' from *Love and Memory: A Garland of Poems 1920-1960* by Rolf Gardiner;

'Living God, you have commanded us to love each other . . .' from *New Prayers for Worship* by Alan Gaunt (John Paul the Preacher's Press, 1972);

extracts from *The Prophet* by Kahlil Gibran Copyright 1923 by Kahlil Gibran and renewed 1951 by Administrators C.T.A. of Kahlil Gibran Estate and Mary G. Gibran Reprinted by permission of Alfred A. Knopf Inc.;

extracts from *My Dear Timothy* © Victor Gollancz 1952, published by Victor Gollancz Ltd. with permission;

extracts from *Joyce Grenfell Requests the Pleasure* by Joyce Grenfell, Copyright © Joyce Grenfell 1976, published by Macmillan, by permission of Richard Scott Simon Limited;

extracts from *A Sparrow's Flight* by Lord Hailsham reproduced by permission of HarperCollins Publishers Ltd;

A & C. Black (Publishers) Limited for permission to quote from Arnold Haskell, *In His True Centre* (1951);

extract from *Tales from Eternity* by Rosemary Haughton reproduced by permission of HarperCollins Publishers Ltd;

extract from *The Prospect Before Her* by Olwen Hufton reproduced by permission of HarperCollins Publishers Ltd;

excepts from the English translation of *Rite of Marriage* © 1969, International Committee on English in the Liturgy, Inc. All rights reserved;

extract from 'Lord Mackay's true valour' by Simon Jenkins (*The Times* 15 June 1996) © Times Newspapers Limited, 1996, by permission of News International Syndication;

'One Flesh' from *Collected Poems* by Elizabeth Jennings, published by Carcanet Press, by permission of David Higham Associates;

extracts from *D. H. Lawrence: Selected Letters* reproduced by permission of Lawrence Pollinger Limited and the Estate of Frieda Lawrence Ravagli;

extract from *A Heart's Odyssey* by Neil Macvicar, published by Michael Russell (Publishing) Ltd, by permission of the author and the publisher;

extract from *Unreasonable Behaviour* by Don McCullin, published by Jonathan Cape, by permission of Random House UK Ltd;

Constable Publishers for permission to quote extracts from *To Keep Faith* by Mary Middleton Murry (1959);

extracts from *Vita and Harold* ed. Nigel Nicolson by permission of Weidenfeld & Nicolson;

extract from *Women Who Love Too Much* by Robin Norwood (New

Acknowledgments

York: G. P. Putnam's and Co., Inc. 1984; London: Arrow Books, 1985) Copyright © 1984, reproduced with the kind permission of the author and of Arrow Books;

two prayers from *Patterns and Prayers for Christian Worship*, © The Baptist Union 1991; used by permission of Oxford University Press;

extract from *The Life of James McNeill Whistler* by E. R. & J. Pennell by permission of the authors' Estate and William Heinemann Ltd;

extracts from *Yeomen of the Cotswolds* by Eleanor Porter & Mary Abbott reproduced with the kind permission of Eleanor Porter (copies available from Penton Grafton, Andover, SP11 0RR);

extracts from *Love and Death* by Llewellyn Powys by permission of the author's Estate and the Bodley Head Ltd;

'Five Domestic Interiors' from *The Winter Man* by Vernon Scannell by permission of the author;

extract from *The Intelligent Woman's Guide to Socialism and Capitalism* by Bernard Shaw, by permission of The Society of Authors on behalf of the Bernard Shaw Estate;

extract from *Fiddler on the Roof* by Joseph Stein Copyright © 1964 by Joseph Stein. Reprinted by permission of Crown Publishers, Inc.;

extracts from *I Married You* by Walter Trobisch quoted with the permission of Editions Trobisch © Editions Trobisch;

extract from *Community and Growth* by Jean Vanier published and copyright 1979 and 1993 by Darton, Longman and Todd Ltd used by permission of the publishers and of Paulist Press;

extracts from *The Essential Mary Webb* ed. Martin Armstrong by permission of Jonathan Cape Ltd;

extract from *The Hearts and Lives of Men* by Fay Weldon with permission of Curtis Brown Ltd. London, (c) Fay Weldon 1987;

extracts from *Marriage* by H. G. Wells by permission of A. P. Watt Ltd on behalf of The Literary Executors of the Estate of H. G. Wells;

extract from 'It's great to get married at 21' by Madeleine Wickham (*Daily Telegraph* 21 April 1997) by kind permission of the author;

extract from 'Marriage? No, I'd rather live' by Petronella Wyatt (*Independent* 28 March 1997) by kind permission of the author;

'For Anne Gregory' from *The Collected Poems of W B Yeats* by permission of A. P. Watt Ltd on behalf of Michael Yeats;

extracts from YOU Magazine: 'How to make a drama out of a Midlife Crisis' by Rob Heyland (19 January 1997) and 'Mother in the Dock' by Katharine Hadley (23 February 1997) by permission of Solo Syndication Limited and YOU Magazine.